QUILL AND BEADWORK OF THE WESTERN SIOUX

Plate 1.   Sioux man in costume

Plate 2. Robe with realistic figures painted by man

QUILL AND BEADWORK
OF THE WESTERN SIOUX

By
CARRIE A. LYFORD

Associate Supervisor of Indian Education

Illustrated with

Photographs and Drawings

Edited by Willard W. Beatty
Chief, Branch of Education (1936—1951)

JOHNSON BOOKS
BOULDER, COLORADO

This edition, first published in 1979, is an unabridged reprint of the 1940 edition issued by the United States Department of the Interior, Bureau of Indian Affairs — Division of Education.

Eleventh Printing 1999

Cover Photograph: Buckskin War Shirt, Brûlé Sioux, by Carmelo Guadagno. Courtesy of Museum of the American Indian, Heye Foundation, New York.

Printed in the United States of America
by
Johnson Publishing Company
1880 S. 57th Court
Boulder, Colorado 80301

CONTENTS

ILLUSTRATIONS

Illustrations through the courtesy of:

(A) American Museum of Natural History, New York City
(D) Denver Art Museum, Denver, Colorado
(E) Bureau of American Ethnology, Washington, D. C.
(O) William C. Orchard, Museum of the American Indian, Heye Foundation, New York City
(T) Julia E. Tuell
(U) United States National Museum, Washington, D. C.

INTRODUCTION

Seventy five, one hundred and two hundred years ago, when visitors from the Old World prepared their baggage for dangerous America, one of its most important items was bright colored beads for the Indians. Traders, explorers, and even officials carried these beads, for they had found that Indian women urged their men to trade for them so that the women might decorate with brilliant patterns the clothing and bags which they made. Such decoration was not a new art. For centuries, the women had been dyeing the quills of the porcupine, sewing them on to garments and bags, and weaving them into belts, much as they later sewed and wove colored beads. This art of quillwork was an American Indian art, practiced nowhere else in the world, and the women gave it up gradually only because beads were so much easier to use.

Any book, therefore, which describes beadwork, should also describe the quillwork, from which the ideas and the designs first came. Quill and beadwork were practiced at some time over all the northern half of the United States and in Canada. Each region had its own styles, colors, and sewing methods, so that an expert can often tell by looking at a piece of beadwork from which tribe it came (or at least from which group of tribes) and about what date it was made. The groups of tribes showing distinct styles are roughly as follows:

Northwestern Plains: Assiniboin, Blackfoot, Nez Perce, etc.

Southern Plains: Kiowa, Comanche, Apache.

Central Plains: Western Sioux, Crow, Cheyenne, Arapaho.

Northeastern Plains: Eastern Sioux, Winnebago.

Southeastern Plains: Omaha, Osage, Ponca, Oto.

Woodland: Iroquois, Algonkin.

To the new student of beadwork who may not have realized how varied the art was, this may seem a large number of divisions. Even the expert will admit that there is much overlapping in design, color, and sewing method, and that frequently one description will do for all. But not always. Therefore the Indian Service is undertaking to publish, if possible, one publication for each of these groups so that Indians and whites, interested in bringing back the old art of a particular tribe, may have as detailed information as possible.

In this publication, we treat not of a group of tribes but of one particular tribe and, in fact, of one portion of it. The Sioux are a very large family who roamed in many directions and learned a variety of customs from their different neighbors. Those who lived at the east, like the Yankton and Sisseton, did beadwork very much like that of the Woodland peoples even further east. Those at the west, the Oglala, were like their western neighbors, Crow, Cheyenne and Arapaho. This book applies in general to the last three tribes as well as the western Sioux. But since the other three are scattered, while the Sioux are a growing tribe on reservations of their own, we have tried here to present designs known to be Sioux, for use in Sioux schools. The purpose of the book is a practical one. Though we have striven for accuracy, our aim has not been an exhaustive scientific study. Rather, it has been to bring together a representative collection of designs and to explain them so that practical workers, both students and teachers, may be able to recognize the bead and quillwork of the western Sioux and to make it for themselves. The art has changed in the past and those who understand its style and uses may use their imaginations to develop it still more, while still keeping it Indian and Sioux.

The material has been assembled from publications of the Bureau of American Ethnology, the American Museum of Natural History, the Museum of the American Indian, the Denver Art Museum, and others, supplemented by such information as could be provided by the older Indians on the reservations. The publication has been reviewed and criticized by Mr. F. H. Douglas of the Denver Art Museum, an authority on Plains handicraft, who generously gave his time to insure the correctness of the information. Dr. Scudder Mekeel, Director of the Laboratory of Anthropology, Santa Fe, (formerly Director of Anthropology, Bureau of Indian Affairs) who has spent much time with the Sioux, offered valued suggestions, as did Dr. Clark Wissler, Curator in Chief, Department of Anthropology of the American Museum of Natural History, New York City. Dr. Ruth Underhill, Associate Supervisor of Indian Education (Anthropology) assisted in preparation of the manuscript. Miss Mabel Morrow, Craft Specialist in the Indian Service, has been liberal in her advice. The many line drawings of Sioux designs are the work of Albert van der Loo of the Branch of Buildings and Utilities of the Bureau of Indian Affairs.

Plate 3. Robe with geometric figures painted by woman

THE WESTERN SIOUX

T HE name Sioux is a shortened French variant of an Ojibwa (Chippewa) word. Nadowe-siw-eg means the Snake-like Ones, or Enemies, which the French spelled Nadowessioux. The people of this great tribe, the second largest in the United States, speak of themselves by a word which means Friends and Allies. Some of them call it Dakota, some Nakota, while the western Sioux, the subject of our discussion, say Lakota. They have, however, accepted "Sioux" as a tribal name.

The roaming ground of this great people, a hundred years and more ago, was the country which is now called North and South Dakota. The Sioux have moved and moved again during their history as shown by the fact that there are even little groups of them in the Carolinas. But the great majority, in historic times, lived on the northern prairies. The French met them, in 1640, in Minnesota. Then came guns and horses which helped their enemies, especially the Ojibwa, to drive them further west but gave to the Sioux the means to follow the buffalo farther and farther out on the Plains. By 1800 they ranged through all the northern country, from Minnesota to the Rockies and south to Iowa, Nebraska and Wyoming.

Over such a wide territory differences naturally developed and, for descriptive purposes, we can divide the Sioux into three groups. The eastern Sioux, who lived along the edge of the Woodlands, include Mdewakanton, the Wahpekute, Wahpeton and Sisseton, now on the Santee and Flandreau reservations. The middle Sioux, once in Iowa and South Dakota, included the Yankton and Yanktonai, now on the Fort Totton, Standing Rock, Crow Creek and Yankton reservations. The western Sioux, the subject of our discussion, are the Teton, "Dwellers on the Prairie" who lived principally along the Missouri but ranged over the Western Plains from Colorado along the Rockies and up into Canada. Their seven bands were the Brulé, (Burned Thighs), Sans Arcs (Without Bows), Sihaspa (Blackfoot, not to be confused with the Algonkin Blackfoot of northern Montana), Minicoujou (Those who Plant Beside the

Stream), Oohenopah (Two Boilings), Oglala (Scattering One's Own), Hunkpa-pa (End of the Circle). As far as can be calculated from census data, there are now over 15,000 of the western Sioux scattered over five South Dakota reservations: Cheyenne River, Lower Brulé, Pine Ridge, Rosebud, and Stand-ing Rock (extending also into North Dakota) with a few at Fort Peck, Montana.

These western Sioux were hunters whose life revolved around the bison (buffalo) and its migrations. In the summer, when the animals pastured on the plains, the Sioux united for great communal hunts to furnish meat and skins for the whole year. In winter, they separated into small groups to shift for themselves until the bison appeared again. The time of the men was fully taken up with hunting, with fighting to retain their hunting territories and their horses, and with the ceremonies which gave strength for these things. Most of the manufactures fell to the women.

The country of the Sioux was cold and they needed a snug house and complete clothing. Because of their frequent wanderings they could have few possessions and these must be light, pliable and unbreakable. To most of these needs, the buffalo itself furnished the answer. They used buffalo hide for their tents, their outer robes, and their food bags; buffalo bladders for small bags; buffalo stomach, sometimes, for cooking pots. Where buffalo hide was too heavy, they substituted elk or deerskin. Skins and other animal products furnished practically their whole equipment, and furnished, too, the materials for their art.

The Problem of Decoration

The problem of decoration was not so simple and the Sioux must have scoured their limited environment for color and ornament. They found they could decorate their leather by cutting and carving it and some of their very old bags are ornamented in this way. More colorful than carving, however, was painting, which they did with earth colors. Both men and women painted on leather but there was a sharp distinction in style. Men painted realistic fig-ures, such as birds, animals and human beings, which they copied from life as well as they could. (Plate 2, Frontispiece.) Women painted only geometric forms, like squares, bands and triangles. (Plates 3 and 4, pp. 10, 13.) Did this distinction arise from some practical basis or was it a ceremonial rule? Sioux women do not know and no research has as yet revealed the answer. The same distinction of realism for men and geometrical figures for women exists in many parts of the world. And in many parts of the world, also, it is men who

Plate 4. Painted parfleche

operate magic, while woman's sphere is the practical household labor. These two facts must have interacted until, now, it is hard to tell which is cause and which is effect. But we can be sure of one thing in looking at any decoration by the western Sioux: if it is geometrical in form, whether it be food bag, tipi ornament, or buffalo robe, it was done by a woman.

Besides painting, women had another form of art not practiced by men. They did the sewing, and even such heavy work as stitching together the heavy buffalo hides that made the tent fell to them. So they developed various kinds of ornament which involved sewing, such as attaching to the leather small decorative objects like seeds, shells, and animal teeth. None of these were colorful and it must have been a major invention for the women of northern North America when someone realized the possibilities of the porcupine quill. This whitish, tubular quill can be dyed with vegetable matter, softened by wetting, and fastened to skins in patterns which resemble embroidery. The porcupine did not live in the Plains where the Sioux finally moved and they must have learned the art of quill embroidery from the east. But they practiced it eagerly,

13

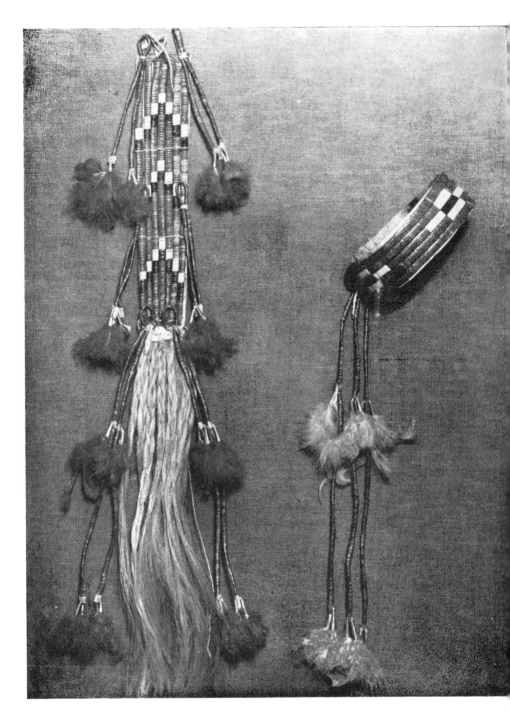

Plate 5. Quilled hair ornament and armlet

trading for the quills with other tribes. Some of the most beautiful pieces of old quill embroidery come from the western Sioux, but they follow the same rule as the women's painting: only geometric design is used. In the later stage of quillwork floral designs make their appearance.

In the nineteenth century, commercial beads were brought to the Plains and the women welcomed them for their bright color and greater ease of handling. Sioux women, in course of time, used various styles and colors of beads, but they always kept to their rule of geometric figures only. Not until very recent years, when beadwork has been made not for the Sioux themselves but for sale to the whites, has this rule been broken.

We can think of western Sioux decoration, then, as having been done mostly upon leather and as being realistic or geometric according to whether it was the work of men or women. The objects so decorated were, of necessity, useful ones. People who moved so frequently could not afford to carry excess baggage and they made nothing for ornamentation except a few bits of personal finery such as armbands. (Plate 5, p. 14.) Their decorations were applied to tools and clothing which they considered a necessity, either for practical use or for the magic which was equally important. Therefore, they could not choose the shape and size of their decorations. These had to conform to the article, whether large or small and no play of fancy must interfere with its usefulness. If we picture the equipment of a Sioux family about 1850, before white influence had grown strong, we shall see what opportunities they had for decoration.

Decoration of Home and Furnishings

Their home was the tipi (Plate 6, p. 16), a conical skin tent on a foundation of three tall poles with others leaning against them. Tipi is, in fact, the Dakota word for dwelling. The tipi was made by women who sewed together ten or twelve tanned buffalo skins in the form of a great circular cape. It was the women's business to take the tipi down when the family moved, to pack it on its poles so that it could be dragged by the horses, and to set it up again at the new camp. It stood 15 or 18 feet high, its sloping walls of smooth, tanned buffalo hide forming an excellent basis for painting. Here the men exercised their art, but under strict rules. A man painted on his tent walls only figures which told of his own magic dreams or his success in battle. To use those of another man was dishonest. The need for a sign to show visitors

Plate 6. Old engraving of Sioux encampment with tipis

who owned the tent, might have been the reason for the man making his special display here. Sometimes women embroidered ornaments on soft buckskin and basted them on the outer walls of the tipi.

Beside the tent, stood the man's shield on a tripod, always turned so that it faced the sun. The shield was made of rawhide, soaked, dried and smoked until it was like wood. This, too, the warrior painted with symbols of his visions. (Plate 24, p. 36.) Inside, he had one more opportunity to use flowing lines of paint on smooth hide. If the family were a wealthy one, owning many skins, they gave their tent an inner lining, reaching halfway up the poles and perhaps all the way around. Tied to the poles and weighed to the floor, it made an excellent windbreak and here the men might let their fancy run freely in decoration. Generally they represented their own exploits and this wall cover often showed vivid pictures of battles and horse stealing.

The furnishings of the tipi were the women's realm. She dug a firepit near the center under the smoke hole, and around it on a foundation of dry grass, she placed the skins and furs which she herself had dressed. Heads to the wall, feet to fire, the family slept on these skins by night. By day, they sat on them, each in his own place, which no one else could use without permission. For daytime use, the woman contrived for each one a backrest, or half chair, light and portable like everything else. It was an ingenious arrangement, looking something like half a hammock and made of willow rods strung together in a parallel position on two rawhide thongs with, perhaps, some bead or quill decoration. It is in the shape of a truncated triangle. It is suspended from a tripod of poles so that a foot or so rests on the ground. (Plate 7, p. 18) Skins might be spread over the backrest to make it more comfortable. The user sits on the horizontal section and leans back against the rest. There might be as many as three or four in a tipi. When the family moved the backrest was rolled up in a small bundle.

With the skins and backrests in position the tipi was as neat as a pin, comfortable, too, with a current of fresh air blowing through the open door and out the smoke hole. All the family's possessions were stowed in their proper places: the man's weapons and his magic bundle at the back, facing the entrance, the woman's cooking things near the door; the clothes and possessions of each member of the family behind his bed, between the backrest and the tipi wall. These possessions were mostly bags and clothing made and decorated by the woman.

17

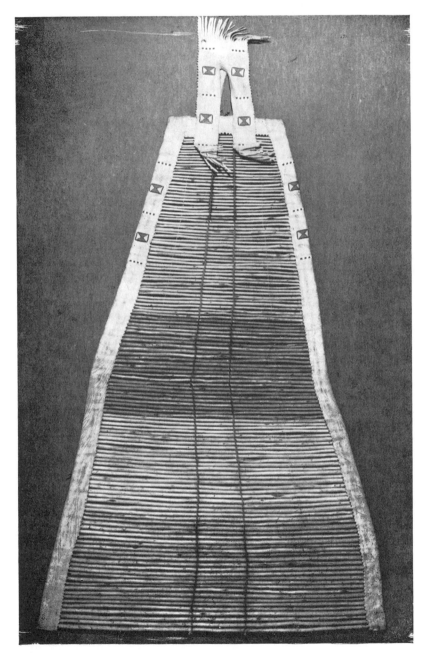

Plate 7. Backrest of willow rods

Decoration of Clothing

Next to the tipi itself, clothing was woman's most important manufacture. It was made of skins, buffalo, elk or deer, tanned by the woman herself with only a modicum of sewing or of cutting. All sewing, in those days, was with awl and sinew, to be described more fully in the following pages. With these tools, a woman could make a strong seam and, on the tent cover, she did so. But the garments were often of whole skins or of two skins, laced together with buckskin thongs. Such lacing is, of course, only a coarse form of sewing, and sinew sewing followed it. For a long time the skins were almost unshaped. Such tailored elements as sleeves and trousers were at first unknown.

The necessary garments for a man were belt, loincloth, moccasins and robe. His belt was a buckskin thong, his loincloth a soft buckskin strip, a foot wide and four or five feet long, passed between the legs and tucked under the belt before and behind. His moccasins had a hard rawhide sole and a soft tanned upper with a tongue and a flap coming up around the ankle. (Plate 8, p. 20.) In summer, he wore no more than moccasins, belt and loincloth; in winter, he added tubular leggings made of single deer or antelope skins, finished with fringe down the outer edge. His upper body he covered with a buffalo robe with the hair left on. He draped this around his body, hair or skin side out, as the weather dictated, and generally with the tail on his right. (Plate 2, Frontispiece.)

Only certain men wore shirts on special occasions, and these were more ponchos than shirts. (Plates 9 and 10, pp. 21-22.) They were made of two dressed skins of deer or antelope. At first these were merely sewed or laced together up the sides and across the shoulders, leaving a hole for the head. They reached to the hips and, from their lower border, the hind legs and tail hung down, both front and back, as decoration. Cape-like sleeves were formed by lacing together the edges of the front legs. In time, the shirt was improved so that it had a yoke across the top and fringe at the seams and border. All of this costume gave plentiful opportunity for decoration, as the following pages will show.

The woman's necessary costume was moccasins, dress and belt. While the man, in summer, might wear only a loincloth, the woman was always completely clothed. Her dress, (Plate 12, p. 24) which came below the knees, was made of two elk hides placed together, with the tails at the top, leaving a hole for the head. The two skins were sewed together across the top so that the tails and the skin on either side of them fell back in flaps, one over the woman's chest, the other over her shoulder blades. Then, beginning

Plate 8. Moccasins

Plate 9. Man's shirt—old style; quill embroidery

at the bottom, the two skins were sewed together up the sides to the point where the hind legs branch out. This left two large, cape-like openings as sleeves. In time, the woman's dress was made with a yoke, as was the man's

21

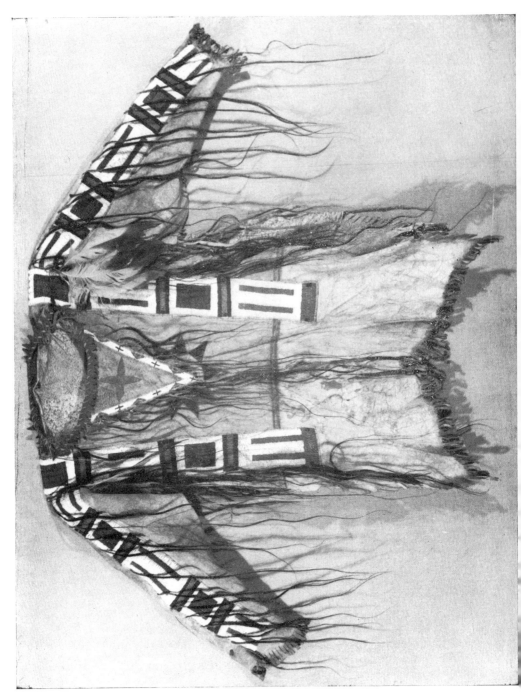

Plate 10. Man's shirt—new style; beaded

shirt. Sioux women came to make very elaborate yokes which sometimes used a whole elk skin. With ceremonial costumes, not meant for every day wear, the yoke was so heavily beaded that the whole dress might weigh from 12 to 16 pounds. But the pattern of the beading still suggested the shape of the ancient costume. The "turtle design," as it is frequently called, has the same lines as the hanging elk tails, before and behind.

The woman, in winter, wore leggings but, because of her long dress, they did not need to reach higher than her knees. There she tied them with thong garters. (Plate 13, p. 25.) Over her dress she wore a buffalo robe, as did the man.

Children wore nothing at all until they were old enough to use the same kind of costumes as their parents.

All this clothing, whether of soft elk skin or heavy buffalo hide, was decorated as elaborately and beautifully as the woman could manage. The scraped inner side of the buffalo robe was as smooth as parchment and well-suited to paint. Both men and women painted their robes, keeping, of course, to their own styles. A man would paint his robe with realistic figures symbolizing his own prowess (Plate 2, Frontispiece), a woman would paint with geometrical figures (Plate 3, p. 10). But beside this, a woman often decorated a robe with rows of laborious quillwork or she added quilled or beaded strips to the painting done by the man.

Plate 11. Beaded blanket strip

On deer and elk skin clothing, where sewing was easier, she spent months of work in attaching bone and shell ornaments, quilled work and, finally, beads. Even when the whites brought red and blue cloth to take the place of buckskin, she did not give up the art but beaded the new garments even more elaborately. Then came bright woolen blankets to take the place of buffalo robes. This was the end of robe painting but not of quilled and beaded ornaments for robes. Women were used to the long strips of such decoration, expanding into discs at regular intervals, which they had used to sew to the tough skin. So they made the same strips to sew to the white man's blankets. (Plate 11, above.)

Plate 12. Woman's dress—with heavily beaded yoke

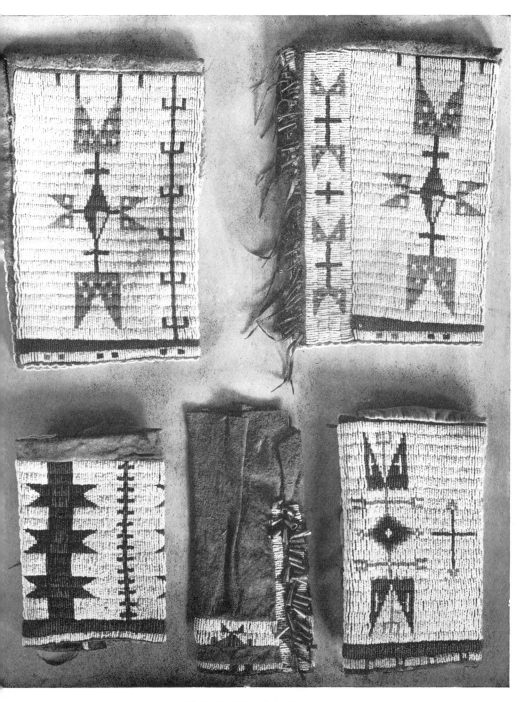

Plate 13. Women's leggings

Decoration of Containers

Next in importance to clothing were the leather bags which substituted for pockets, for trunks and, in some cases, for dishes. Some of these were made of soft, dressed leather on which embroidery was possible; others of tough rawhide where the choice was paint or nothing. The containers which were embroidered are listed below.

1. The pocket bag. (*Plate 14, below.*) A soft bag, perhaps six inches square, with decorative fringe, which served instead of a pocket. Worn at the belt and used by men for tobacco or paint, by women for sewing materials.

2. The pipe bag. (*Plate 15, p. 27.*) A soft bag, a foot or more long by about six inches wide, heavily fringed at the bottom. Used by every family head to hold his ceremonial pipe and kept on the floor at the back of the tipi below his magic bundle.

3. The saddle bag, single or double. Soft. The single type (*Plates 17 and 18, pp. 29-30*), usually made in matched pairs, is a large, rectangular bag about 24 x 16 x 4 inches. This type was hung from the saddle on either side of the horse or hung up in the tipi to hold clothing and other household articles. The flat double type is about 48 x 12. (*Plate 16, p. 28.*) It is made by sewing two rectangular pieces all around their edges except for a section on or near one long side. Things to be carried are inserted through the opening into either end of the bag, which hangs over the horse's back behind the saddle.

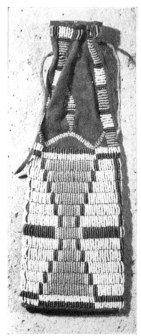

Plate 14. Pocket bag

4. The strike-a-light bag (*Plate 19, p. 31*) worn at a man's belt on journeys and used to carry flints for making fire. Later, it served very well for government ration tickets and was made of stiff leather, perhaps to keep them uncrumpled. It was 3 to 5 inches long and 2 to 4 inches wide.

5. The knife sheath. Stiff. (*Plate 20, p. 31.*) A late development, hung at the belt and meant to carry a knife.

Plate 15.   Pipe bags

Plate 16. Saddle bag, double

6. The medicine bag. This could take such various forms that it can hardly be classified. It might be made of a small animal skin with the fur either on or off, or of a bladder, or it might be of soft, dressed skin. Its purpose was to hold the objects which a man had been told in a dream to collect and keep as his personal magic. It hung on a tripod at the back of the tipi and was opened only on important occasions.

The heavier articles were all made of rawhide: the war bonnet case; the pouch; the tub-like mortar for pounding the berries; the parfleche, a large rectangle, folded like an envelope and used to carry pounded meat and berries; and in later years the trunk. (*Plate 4*, p. 13.) The rough articles were left undecorated, but the smooth ones, like the parfleche and trunk, the woman always painted with her own geometric designs.

The containers, other than leather, were a few wooden dishes hollowed out of a solid block by gouging and burning.

If bags and containers were necessary, weapons and horse trappings were equally so. Every member of the family might have a decorated saddle blanket and bridle. The men might have bow cases and quivers; later, gun cases.

Decoration of Ceremonial Property

Beyond these everyday things came the ceremonial property. Any important man had dreamed, after fasting and prayer, of some powerful being, like an animal or plant, with more than human knowledge. This guardian spirit had given him magic power and bidden him collect certain objects which should express it and which he was to keep with great reverence. Usually, he wrapped them in a rough skin bundle made by himself, but sometimes the woman might add her beaded or quilled decoration. Probably the

28

man had a pipe which was not for mere relaxation but to honor guests, and to smoke during deliberations. For the pipe, too, the woman did her part by sheathing the stem in quill or beadwork. There might be, too, a cane or a feather fan to use in ceremonial dances, their handles sheathed in the same way.

In later years, as Sioux religion changed, the idea persisted that sacred objects should be beautifully quilled or beaded. When some of the Sioux took up the peyote cult in which, during reverent ceremonies, they obtain a trance by eating a particular cactus root, their feather fans and their rattles were elaborately beaded. Even before that, they had been beautifying their Christian mission churches with altar cloths, stoles, hymn books, and church hangings all of beadwork.

At home, the women had had certain ceremonial articles of their own. It was their custom to save the navel cord of a firstborn child and, for its safe keeping, they made a little buckskin bag, often shaped like a turtle,

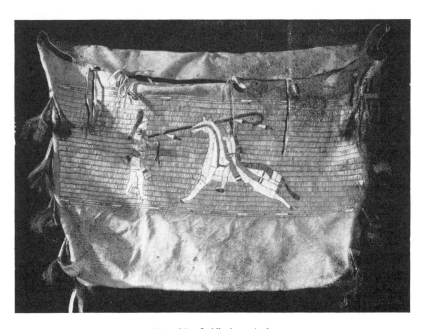

Plate 17. Saddle bag, single

29

Plate 18. Saddle bag, single, one of a pair

Plate 19. Strike-a-light bag

beaded or quilled. Within it, the cord was packed in milkweed and herbs; and the baby, when he grew up, wore it at his belt on the left side as a charm. The cradle in which the baby was strapped was often a gift to the mother and ornamented with a beaded hood. A handsome gift like that called for a gift in exchange, sometimes a horse. (Plate 21, p. 32.)

Not every family owned all the objects mentioned above, and where they were owned, they were not always decorated. But it was the pride of a Sioux housewife to decorate every article of her scant but necessary equipment. Virtue in a woman meant industry, and industry was often gauged by the amount of porcupine quilling she had done on heavy buffalo robes, and on shirts and moccasins that wore out and must be quilled again. Great must have been the urge for decoration which kept a woman at this laborious means of attaining it.

She worked, not only for her own family, but on ceremonial gifts to be given away on great occasions. The custom of the "give away" was a fundamental one with this wandering people who had no storage for goods and who prized honor and generosity more than caution and thrift. A family honored one of its members at any important period of his life by a feast at which gifts were distributed not to the individual who was being honored but to friends and neighbors so that the recipients might sing his praises. A father gave such a feast for his son at the name giving ceremony, the killing of the first buffalo calf, the first war party. He gave one for his daughter when he wished to present her with an elkskin dress and have her specially admonished as to the duties of an upright maiden. He gave one for himself when he wished to show by his generosity that he feared poverty no more than he feared his enemy.

At such ceremonies horses were the special wealth distributed, but many a woman delighted to lavish her work on a quilled or beaded article and give it away to show her industry and generosity. Her reward was praise or perhaps an equal gift when one of her neighbors

Pl. 20. Knife sheath

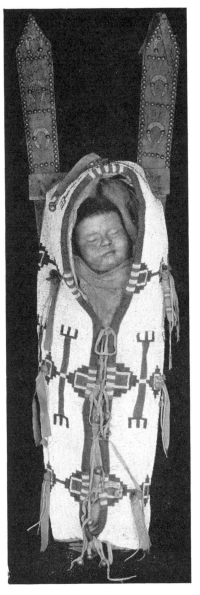

Plate 21. Sioux cradle

held a similiar ceremony. Thus, handsome quilled and beaded articles were, in one sense, a medium of exchange, a sign of high standing.

Numbers of these articles are to be seen today, ly'ng inert on museum shelves. In such an arrangement, the hard outlines of the geometrical figures often look harsh. The leggings, the shirts, the saddle bags, the beaded robes would look very different seen on a living man seated on a galloping horse. It is in such motion that we should think of the brilliant, severe figures which formed the art expression of the Sioux woman.

SKINS AND SINEW

IN former days, when the Sioux band was rich, they said their camp was "full of meat and hides." The meat they ate up, but the hides were permanent wealth. From these, their women could manufacture almost anything that might be needed, from a dwelling to a baby carrier. Bison hide, as we have said, was by far the most important but it was too heavy for many uses. From time to time the hunters also brought in deer, elk, moose, beaver, antelope, mountain lion, coyote, badger, ermine, muskrat, and even rabbit.

All these skins the women put to use with the greatest care and economy. Elk and deer skins were used for clothing, a whole elk skin serving for the dress of a small girl and two skins for a woman. Leftover scraps of elk and deer skin were used for moccasin uppers, while scraps from the tipi made moccasin soles. Other scraps made fringes or small bags. Even old dried pieces of skin were softened and used again and again. Hides of the furry animals were tanned with the fur on and used for bedding. A huge bison hide was, of course, the best of all; but hides of wolf and beaver were very useful. Hides of small animals like mountain lion and coyote were sometimes used whole for bags or quivers. Soft fur like that of rabbit and ermine could be used in strips for decoration.

Preparation of Skins

The dressed skins varied widely both in texture and in the degree of finish which they were given. The skin used in shields was hard and resistant; the rawhide used for parfleche bags, though thinner, was stiff but could be bent without cracking; the finest buckskin was pure white, soft, and as smooth as a delicate cotton fabric. Some of the leather was so perfectly tanned that it is in as good condition today as it was one hundred years ago.

Plate 22. Skin preparation. Staking it out

An Indian camp presented a scene of great activity when skins were being prepared for use. A large group of workers usually participated in the dressing of skins for much labor was involved. If a green hide was to be tanned with the hair on, it was stretched and staked to the ground, hair side down. If a hide was dry it was necessary to soak it before staking it out. The tissue was removed and the skin reduced to a uniform thickness by scraping it on the fleshy side with an adz-like tool, called a flesher, which was made from bone or antler with a stone and later an iron blade. (*Plates 22 and 23, pp. 34-35.*)

The skin thus prepared was known as rawhide and was used for moccasin soles, parfleche cases, or drums. Hides prepared in this way were hard, quite stiff, and very durable. If an unusually thick or hard rawhide was desired, the skin was alternately soaked and dried over a slow, smoky fire.

Plate 23. Skin preparation. Scraping

Plate 24. Painted rawhide shield

If a soft flexible skin was desired, further treatment was necessary. Specially prepared mixtures of brains, eggs, cooked ground-up liver, spleen, and fat from the animal or mixtures of vegetable products were rubbed into the hide on the flesh side. In recent times a strong soap solution has been used for this purpose. When the hide was well-saturated with the mixture, it was dried then soaked in warm water and rolled up in a tight bundle. If the hide had not been well-staked down to the ground before the process of curing was begun, it became much shrunken, and it was necessary to stretch it after curing had been completed. A breaking or softening process was therefore necessary. This was accomplished by alternately soaking the hide in warm water and by pulling with hands and feet, by pulling down over a rounded post, or by two persons stretching it. Sometimes the skin was pulled rapidly through a small opening to give greater softness or it was rubbed on both sides with rough stones until the tissues had been broken and it had been softened up. The well-tanned skin was restored to nearly its original size, thoroughly softened, and smooth.

To prepare skins for war shields, a heavy piece of hide from the shoulder or neck of a buffalo might be chosen, staked down on the bottom of a hole six or eight inches deep, and covered with dirt. A fire was kept burning over it for several days. After such processing a skin would be shrunken and very thick, suitable for the purpose it was to serve. (*Pl. 24, p. 36.*)

Cleaning Dressed Skins

Articles made of skin soil easily, but Indian women are able to clean a well-tanned skin satisfactorily by the use of chalk, porous bone, native clay, or porous rock. Wet white clay is rubbed on the skin and brushed off when dry. The Blackfoot Indians cleaned tanned skins with a piece of fungus.

Decline in the Use of Skins

Even before the eighteenth century, manufactured cloth had become available to the Indians in the eastern part of the country. Heavy woolen blankets and coarse strouding gradually replaced the robes of skin. Calico became popular for women's dresses and men's shirts. By 1850 the Plains Indians were using woolen and cotton cloth as robes in place of skins or combining it with skin on various articles. Flannelette or eiderdown and calico served to line or bind and finish the edges of articles made of skins. Red, blue, or green flannel was frequently used as a basis for beaded bands, belts, and feathered war bonnets.

Sinew

Before commercial threads and steel needles were introduced to them, the Indians sewed with sinew thread, using an awl made of a sharp splinter of bone or horn or a thorn of the buffalo berry bush to puncture holes in the material to be sewed. Later a steel awl or a nail, ground to a point, was substituted.

Sinew was obtained from buffalo, elk, moose, or other animals. There was usually an ample supply of sinew in the camp after the hunts, for every part of the animal was preserved by the Plains Indians for later use. Today sinew is commonly obtained from a beef or calf. Horse sinew is also valued as the fibers are long and easy to roll. The sinew for sewing was taken from the large tendon which lies along each side of the back bone, beginning just back of the neck joint and extending for about three feet. This tendon is removed as intact as possible from the body so that the threads of sinew will be long. The short piece of tendon found under the shoulder blade of the cow provided a thick cord of sinew, several lengths of which were sometimes twisted together for use as a bow string.

While still moist, the tendon is cleaned by scraping it thoroughly with a piece of flint or bone. Before too dry, the tendon is softened by rubbing it together between the hands, after which the fibers of sinew can be stripped off easily with an awl or piece of flint. If the tendon is not prepared soon after it is taken from the body or if the natural glue is not removed, it becomes stiff and dry and must be soaked until freed from the glue which clings to it. Then it is hammered and softened until the fibers can be stripped off readily.

As the fibers are stripped off in lengths of from one to three feet, they are moistened with saliva and twisted by rubbing them against the knee with a quick motion until they have acquired the proper degree of elasticity. For convenience in using, the experienced beadworker often strips off enough of the sinew to braid in a loose plait from which a fiber can easily be drawn out as needed. The sinew is carefully wrapped until it is to be used.

For use in sewing, a soft end of the sinew is wet with saliva, twisted to a fine point and allowed to dry stiff and hard so it may be slipped easily through the awl holes in the skins. Several pieces of sinew may be prepared in this way before embroidery work begins. While working, the women keep the strip of sinew moistened by applying salvia with the finger tips.

Though sinew can be kept indefinitely, and the thrifty beadworker usually has a supply on hand, it is easier to use when fresh as it has a tendency to become brittle when dry unless the natural glue has all been removed. If too dry it can be soaked in warm water to restore its flexibility. However, for strong, flexible, permanent thread, care must be taken to remove the natural glue by immediate and adequate soaking of the tendon.

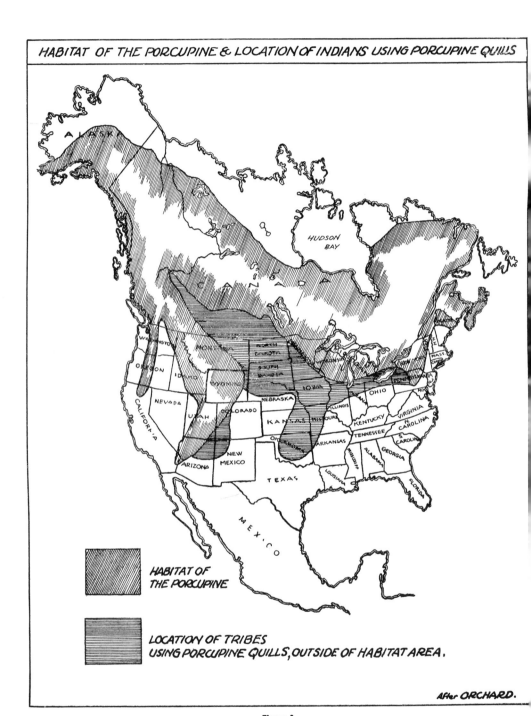

HABITAT OF THE PORCUPINE & LOCATION OF INDIANS USING PORCUPINE QUILLS

HABITAT OF
THE PORCUPINE

LOCATION OF TRIBES
USING PORCUPINE QUILLS, OUTSIDE OF HABITAT AREA.

After ORCHARD.

Figure 1

PORCUPINE QUILL WORK

PORCUPINE quillwork was the forerunner of beadwork and had been developed to a high degree of artistic perfection before the first European beads were brought to this country. Pieces of quillwork known to be over two hundred years old have been collected. Beginning about 1800 the introduction of beads provided a decorative material which supplemented and tended to replace quills.

The home of the American porcupine is Canada and Alaska, with extensions into the northern United States, chiefly into mountainous country. Cne of these extensions in the east reaches down through the White Mountains, Adirondacks and Alleghanies, including parts of Vermont, New York and Pennsylvania. In plains and prairie country, porcupines are not found and the line of their southern range passes through the Great Lakes country and up into Alberta. Another extension reaches down along the Rocky Mountains as far south as New Mexico and a narrower one along the Cascade Range, including parts of Washington, Oregon and northern California. (*Figure1*, *p. 40.*)

Porcupine quills were used for decoration throughout this country and also in some of the intervening area, notably the Plains, where the quills had to be obtained by trade.

The quill of the porcupine is a round hollow tube which terminates in a barbed point at one end. It is white for about four-fifths of its length, ending in a brownish gray tip. However, the quills differ in length, thickness, and stiffness, varying from one to four inches in length and from one-sixteenth to three thirty-seconds of an inch in width. The quillworkers sometimes divided them into four sizes: the largest and coarsest which come from the tail of the porcupine; the next largest from the back; the slender, delicate quills from the neck; and the finest which come from the belly. The fine quills were used for delicate work such as found on old moccasins. In some of the old embroidery such fine quills were used that the work resembles moose hair embroidery, from which it can be distinguished, however, by the shiny surface of the quills. The medium-sized and coarser quills were used on larger pieces. The Indian women kept the quills, sorted as to size, in cases which might be made of a portion of the intestine of an elk, a buffalo bladder, or in specially made rawhide boxes. The bladder cases were sometimes decorated with bead embroidery. Very rarely, split bird quills were substituted for those of the porcupine.

Men hunted the porcupine with bows and arrows, driving it into a hole or up a tree where it was helpless. According to some accounts, they pulled out the quills without killing the animal but, more usually, the porcupine was killed, roasted, and eaten while the quills were carefully plucked, sorted for size, and kept for decorative purposes or for trade.

After the coming of the white man, who brought with him brightly colored manufactured beads, quillwork gradually disappeared in many parts of the United States. With it went the knowledge of the source and methods of preparation of many of the vegetable dyes with which the quills were colored. Aniline dyes, carried west by the traders, were substituted for native dyes after about 1880.

Laws to prevent the extermination of the porcupine have been enacted in some sections. If the quills were collected where there is an abundance of porcupines and distributed to the native workers in other sections of the country, much of the old art might yet be preserved.

Dyes

Each areas had its local vegetable dyes. There remain no detailed descriptions of their use but old people state that quills and dye materials were simply boiled together until a good color resulted. Colors known to have been used by the western Sioux were:

Red. Buffalo berry (Lepargyraea) or squaw berry (Virburnum) were used in producing red dye. Buffalo berry, having more juice and less seed, required fewer berries for a good bright color. Either red could be brightened by adding dock root which must be from the "mother" plant, recognizable by the flowers.

Yellow. Wild sunflower (Ratibida columnaris) or cone flower petals were boiled with pieces of decayed oak bark or with the roots of cattail.

The Sioux are said to have had another yellow dye from the bark of a certain pine tree found only in the Black Hills. It is possible, too, that they used the wolf moss (Evernia vulpina) and the fruit and root of the female plant of the curled dock (Rumox crispus) in common with their neighbors the Cheyenne, whose quillwork is similar to theirs.

Black. Wild grapes (Vitis sp.), hickory nuts (Hicoria ovate) or black walnuts (Juglans nigra). Nuts of either sort were used only when grapes were not obtainable, for they gave a brownish color rather than a deep black. They were gathered while the shell was soft, spread in the sun, and occasionally sprinkled with water until they turned black.

Plate 25. Quilled fringed bag

These three colors, with their shades and combinations, were the only ones known to have been used by the Sioux before the whites came. When trade goods arrived, the Sioux made blue by boiling blue cloth with their quills. In reservation days, the cloth often came from blankets issued by the Government. Trade also brought aniline dyes and these took the place of old vegetable colors, so that few of the latter can now be found or even remembered.

Quill Techniques

Quills were washed well, preferably in a soapy bath, before being used. For embroidery work the quill worker moistened them by holding them in her mouth in order to soften them. She generally kept a number in one cheek with points protruding from her lips, pulling out a quill as it was

Figure 2. Quill wrapping without thread fastening

Figure 3. Quill wrapping on hair

needed. The warmth and moisture of the mouth were effective in softening the quills. It was thought that the saliva contained some special property that made them more pliable. After they had been softened in this way the quills were flattened by drawing between the finger nails or teeth. After the quills were sewn down they might be further smoothed by rubbing with a "quill flattener," a special instrument made of a smooth flat bone.

American Indians used quills in four principal ways which have been called wrapping, braiding or plaiting, sewing, and weaving. Not all of these were found throughout the country and each, in its own region, had numbers of variations. The western Sioux practiced only the first three. Weaving, the last method, is practiced chiefly by the Canadian Woodland Indians to the northeast of the Sioux.

Wrapping. This is the simplest method of applying quills and is used to cover long, slender objects, like pipe stems, or strands of leather fringe. The method was to bend the moistened quills around the object to be decorated, beginning with several overlapping rounds of wrapping to cover the end of the quill. As new quills were added, their ends were twisted around the old ones with a half turn which was concealed by the next wrapping. *Figure 2, above.*) Such covering is common on the rawhide fringe which often decorates the bottom of a Sioux bag. Its strands are six to eight inches long, an eighth to a quarter inch wide, and are joined together at the bottom as well as the top. (*Plate 25, p. 43.*) Wrapping was used, too, on hanks of hair (horse, buffalo, or human), which were sewed down on a shirt in straight lines, single or double. (*Figure 3.*) Or, the wrapped hair was twisted into a rosette

Plate 26. Detail of quilled vest

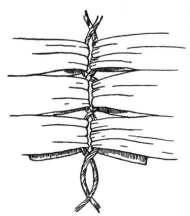

Figure 4. Quill wrapping of fringe fastened with thread

and, while being twisted, was sewed to a piece of buckskin by passing the sinew through the loops of the quills. (*Plate 26, p. 45.*)

The twisting in of the new quills, in this simplest wrapping, was somewhat clumsy and often, especially on fringe strands, the ends were smoothly held by a sinew thread. (*Figure 4.*) The thread was fastened down the entire length of a strand at the back where it would not show. The end of each quill was caught under it, then the quill was wrapped around the strand as far as it would go and new quills were slipped under the thread as needed. This is the method found most commonly on old Sioux bags, such as that illustrated in plate 15, page 27.

Variously colored quills were sometimes used and arranged so as to form a pattern on the fringe. It is possible also to use a string in the wrapping of pipestems, passing it down the back of the stem and knotting it around the quills in a variety of ways. But as far as evidence shows, none of these were used by the western Sioux.

Plaiting. The most elaborate Sioux method of decorating a pipestem was to wrap it, not with single quills but with strips of quill plaiting. (*Plate 28.*) To make this (*Figure 5, p. 47*) a woman held the pipestem she was decorating in her lap and stretched two sinew threads taut between it and a small stick stuck in the ground or in her moccasin. She kept the strings separated by a spreader of bone or wood, about three inches wide, notched at both ends. Taking a moist quill from her mouth, she placed it across both threads, underneath them, and held it in place with the forefinger of her right hand. In this position, the pointed end of the quill extended to the right about half an inch and the butt end to the left the remainder of its length. With the first finger of her left hand she took the butt and brought it up over and down between the threads, over the left thread and under the right, so that it extended to the right. Again with her left forefinger, she reached over to the right and pulled the quill over the right thread and under the left. In this way she wove it to and fro until only a half inch of the butt was left, extending to the right. Then she took a new quill from her mouth and placed it as she had the first. She passed it over the left thread and under the right, and, as it went down between the two threads, her right thumb forced the remaining butt of

46

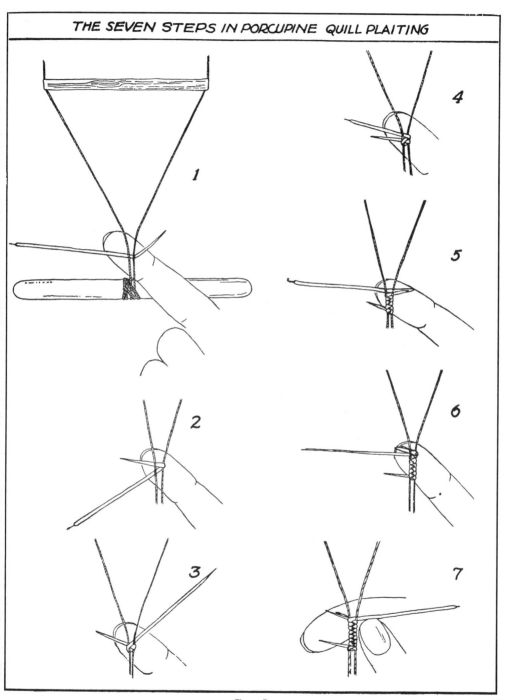

Figure 5

the first quill over the right and between the two threads where it was caught by the new quill coming up from the left.

She continued in this way until two or three inches of plaiting had been made. If she planned to make a pattern and not a mere plaiting of one color, she must now roll her completed plaiting around the pipestem to see how the pattern would fit and where new colors must be introduced. Old pipestems show elaborate figures of men and geometrical forms made in this way.

As a rule, the process is as described above. There are several variations, but the result attained is the same. Very occasionally, instead of one quill, two quills were used, one starting from the right and one from the left and weaving across each other. We can distinguish cne-quill plaiting by the fact that the completed strip presents two series of tall opposed triangles, alternating point and base all along the strip. (*Figure 6, p. 49.*) In two-quill work, the interweaving produces a series of small diamonds down the middle cf the strip. The same effect is seen in sewing with one or two quills, to be described below. (*Figure 8E, p. 50.*)

Plate 27. Plaited quillwork applied to pipe stem

SEWING

No awl hole was ever made in a quill since this would split it. The method of attachng quills to buckskin or cloth was to run a thread through the material and then wind or fold the moistened quills over the thread. While moist the quills could be bent into any shape desired and then wou'd dry firm in that position. Before following the various ways in which quills could be applied, it is of interest, therefore, to consider the stitching process and to know how

Figure 6. One-quill plaiting

the sinew, which was to hold the quills, was actually run through the buckskin.

Stitches. Anyone unused to sinew would be amazed at the fineness of the stitches which were made with this apparently coarse material and without a needle. Not only were they small but they passed only part way through the thick buckskin, so that on the wrong side nothing appeared. Indian women used three main varieties of stitch which Orchard, who has made the authoritative study of quillwork, calls the spotstitch, backstitch, and loopstitch. In the spotstitch, *Figure 7A*, which is the easiest, the sinew passed in and out of the holes in a straight or curved line like thread in a modern running stitch. The exposed portion of the stitch of sinew served as a loop through which the quills were drawn, either tightly or loosely as desired. The moist quills could easily be bent to form curves between the stitches, making it possible to embroider on skins the fine designs and delicate figures characteristic of the Woodland Indians. In the *backstitch*, *Figure 7B*, which was firmer, each stitch pointed up and back at a sharp angle. As the thread was carried forward, it caused the leather to twist and hold the quill tight. The back stitch was much used in early work and even in the oldest specimens is rarely found to have pulled out. The *loopstitch*, *Figure 7C*, was very much like a modern buttonhole stitch. As the awl went into the skin, it was pointed upward; the sinew was drawn through and then looped under itself before entering the next hole.

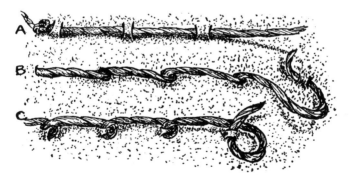

Figure 7. Diagrams: A, spotstitch; B, backstitch; C, loopstitch

49

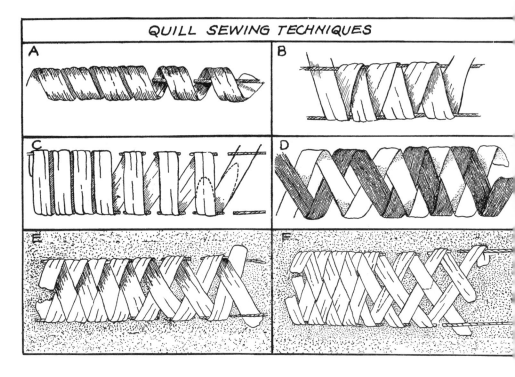

Figure 8. A, one thread; B, two thread; C, one quill, straight; D, two quill, diagonal; E, two quills; F, three quills. C and F show method of splicing (dotted lines)

Stitches of these three sorts can be recognized when quillwork is pulled apart but, in the finished product, they are never seen for each stitch, as it was made, passed over a quill which was then bent to cover it. The quills might be placed in various ways, of which two are outstanding. In the first, which is practiced largely by Eastern Indians, a single quill is twisted around a single thread. (*Figure 8A, above.*) This permits of a curving, flexible line and eastern quillwork is easily recognized because of the delicate tracery thus produced. The eastern Sioux, the Iroquois, and other Woodland Indians practiced this single thread sewing which also spread to some western groups, like the Shoshoni. But the western Sioux, with whom we are concerned, used it little.

Their typical sewing method was to use not one line of stitching but two, more or less parallel, with the quills folded back and forth across them. (*Figure 8B, p. 50.*) The result looks like plaiting because the process is essentially the same. The two threads, instead of being stretched taut in the air, are stitched through buckskin and the stitching goes on at the same time as the folding of the quills. But we can distinguish the tall triangles of one-quill work and the diamonds of two-quill work, as well as further variations which firm stitching makes possible. It is obvious that this two-line arrangement does not lend itself to the slender and flexible figures possible with one line of stitching. Its effect is that of broad lines and bands, straight or but slightly curving, and this banded appearance is characteristic of western Sioux quillwork. Plate 26, p. 45, in which both the curving and the banded styles appear, makes this difference evident.

One-Quill Sewing. The Sioux woman, though committed to the use of two lines of stitching rather than one, had still a choice as to the number of quills she would use simultaneously. The simplest method she employed was to use one quill which she folded to and fro, from one line of stitching to the other, holding the same side of the quill always uppermost. Figure 8C, p. 50, shows this method starting at the left and resulting in a series of parallel lines. (*Plate 27, p. 48.*)

But the quill might also be folded so that, as it passed to and fro across the two lines of stitching, it had first one of its sides uppermost, then the other. This is actually the same movement as in plaiting and produces the same result: two series of tall triangles. Figure 8B, p. 50, shows a band made in this way, the work starting at the left. Finished examples of this style of work appear in Plates 28 and 29, pp. 51-53. If the quill were backed by another

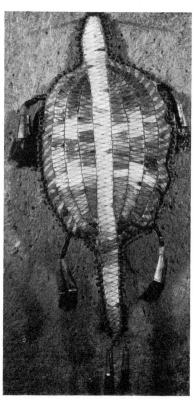

Plate 28.   Quilled turtle amulet

of different color, the triangles would show the two colors alternately and this was sometimes done. (*Plate 25, p. 43, and Figure 8D, p. 50.*)

Two, Three and Four Quills. In Figure 8E, p. 50, two quills are used, one starting under the top thread, one under the bottom thread. They cross each other as they go to and fro so that the quill which actually shows in the finished work is now one of them, now the other. The effect is a series of short triangles along one edge of the band. But the two quills can be interwoven at every crossing so that a part of each always shows. Here the effect is a series of diamonds. Plate 28, p. 51 shows this in the central band. Three quills, interwoven, are shown in Figure 8F, p. 50.

Splicing. The quills being short, it was necessary frequently to insert new ones without showing any break in the surface. The Sioux method was to lay the point of a new quill inside the fold of the last quill where a stitch would hold both of them down. The end of the last quill then came at the back of the band where it would not show, and the next fold was made by the new quill alone. This is shown by dotted lines in Figures 8C and 8F, p. 50.

Design

A rather narrow band is the main unit in Sioux quillwork. The narrow band is made necessary by the shortness of the quills which does not permit the making of wide areas of embroidery. The designs are created either by varying the color in each band according to a regular formula, or by building up larger designs by placing a number of bands close to each other so that the sections of design on each band unite to form the complete pattern. The bands may be straight or worked into discs. The designs are combinations of stripes, bars, squares, oblongs, triangles or circles. In sewn work discs appear especially as tipi ornaments, on the front or back of shirts, and on moccasins and bags. Straight bands of sewn work are used on headdresses, shirt sleeves or shoulders, leggings and moccasins. Bands of wrapped quilling are used mostly on pipe bag fringes but also appear on horse trappings and tipi ornaments. Bands of plaited quilling are used on pipe stems and soft fringes.

Some time after 1800, the Cree began to migrate westward from the area of the Great Lakes. The Cree were among those Woodland Indians who have been mentioned as using the single line and the flexible, curved design and their favorite patterns were symmetrically arranged groups of leaves and flowers such as they had been used to carving on birchbark. The influence of the Cree may have seeped down through various Canadian tribes until it touched the western Sioux for these Indians also began to attempt floral groups in quillwork. Their early designs were somewhat stiff and formalized

Plate 29. Quilled vest

Plate 30.   Detail of quilled gauntlet

(*Plate 30, above*); later designs more realistic (*Plate 26, p. 45*). Often, the
old geometric design was combined with the later vegetable patterns. (*Plate
29, p. 53.*)

The traditional origin of quillwork is explained by a legend of the Oglala Sioux of a mythical "double woman," who came in a dream to some woman who was a twin to teach her the use of quills. She in turn taught other women how to use the quills, and associations of quillworkers or quilling societies were formed. They met at regular intervals to exhibit and talk over their work and explain how they did it. Feasts were held and gifts were distributed. The quill designs made by each woman were considered her personal property and were not copied; for her designs were those which she was supposed to have dreamed and to which she could claim ownership.

The older members of the tribes valued quillweaving and embroidery more highly than beadwork, and a few of the older women on the Sioux reservations continue to use porcupine quills on their moccasins and costumes. Indeed, there are signs of a revival of interest in quillwork at this time.

BEADWORK

EVEN before the European travelers came to this country with glass beads crude native beads wrought out of shell, stone, bones of fish and animals, deer hoofs or toes, teeth, and seeds had been in use. From such materials Indian necklaces, pendants, belts, costume fringes, and other decorative objects. The Sioux and other Plains Indians made a tubular bone bead which has always been popular for use on breast-plates.

In addition to beads, other ornaments have been similarly used on Sioux costumes. The milk teeth of the elk, threaded on a skin thong or piece of fringe, was the most costly of ornaments for the dress of the Sioux woman of rank. A bead cut from bone to imitate the tooth of the elk has been used in recent years on the woman's ceremonial dress as a substitute for elk's teeth because it is now illegal in many areas to kill the animal.

Most of these native beads had been prepared at such great expenditure of time and labor that they were eagerly replaced by the bright, manufactured beads of glass and metal in varied forms and sizes which were brought into the country from Europe. Most glass beads are Venetian or Bohemian. The variation in the types of beads is reflected in the products made by the Indians.

From about 1800 to 1840 a large opaque irregular china bead came into use on the Plains. It was known as the pony bead because it was brought in by the pony pack trains. The pony bead was made in Venice. It was about $\frac{1}{8}$ inch in diameter, about twice as large as the beads used later. White and a medium sky blue were the colors in which the pony beads were commonly used. Black pony beads also appear in the old pieces. A few deep buff, light and dark red, and dark blue pony beads have also been noted.

The pony beads were first used by Plains Indians on bands to decorate skin robes, shirts, pipe bags, cradles, saddle bags, moccasins, and the head bands on war bonnets. The bands were usually less than six inches wide and

were solidly beaded with designs consisting of bars, tall triagnles and concentric squares and diamonds similar to the early quillwork designs. Examples of the early work with pony beads are to be found on the articles collected by Lewis and Clark in 1805 and they are mentioned in the journal of their expedition.

About 1840 a smaller, round, opaque Venetian bead known as a "seed" bead came into use and has continued popular to the present time. (Plate 31 shows examples of pony and seed beads.) The seed beads have always been sold in a great variety of colors in bunches of five or six strings each, the strings varying in length from four to six inches. There are four or five bunches to the pound. The beads come in three sizes varying from one-sixteenth to three-sixteenths of an inch in diameter. The delicacy of the pattern to be embroidered determined the size of bead chosen. Because the beads were partly made by hand they were somewhat irregular in shape and the old beadworker found it necessary to exercise care in using those of equal size.

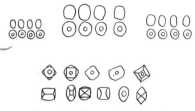

Figure 9. Shapes of trade beads

The colors of the old beads were richer and softer than the colors of the modern beads, though the latter are more regular in size. The small seed beads continue in favor with the conservative Sioux beadworkers. (*Figure 9.*)

The first use of the seed beads was to make bands, very like those made with pony beads and often with the same general pattern. They were put on hip-length leggings, skin robes, pipe bags, cradles, and saddle bags. Not only the Sioux but the Crow and the Blackfoot made similar bands which appear in old pictures from the whole region.

Toward 1860, when settlers began to crowd into the Sioux country, beadwork took a sudden spurt. Beads were to be had in quantity and women began to decorate all their possessions not in bands but in huge all-over patterns. They put these on garments, (*Plates 8, 10, 12, 13, pp. 20, 22, 24, 25,*) bags of all sizes and shapes, (*Plates 14, 15, 19, 20, 25, pp. 26, 27, 31, 43,*) horse furniture, (*Plates 16, 17, 18, 32, pp. 28, 29, 30, 59,*) toys, tipi furnishings, and ceremonial objects. They made beadwork not only for themselves but for the whites who often furnished the garment to be decorated and dictated the style. Also, they saw new objects belonging to the whites and used them, at least insofar as these coincided with their own taste. This second period is marked by a profusion of beadwork and a sudden change of style to be discussed further below. As it advanced, the traders began to bring in Bohemian (Czechoslovakian) beads, which were a trifle darker than the Venetian and inclined to a slightly bluish tinge. One acquainted with both types of beads can recognize this coloring and guess at the date of an article. About 1870 there began to appear translucent beads and, toward 1885, glass beads colored silver or gilt and faceted throughout. There was a huge variety of colors and sizes coming not only from Venice and Bohemia but from France and England.

Very fine lustrous cut glass beads are to be found on some of the finest old pieces of embroidery. As these fine translucent beads are no longer obtainable at the traders' stores, the few that have been kept by the beadworkers are carefully treasured and are used only on choice pieces that are to serve a special purpose.

By 1900 the great period of beadwork was over. Skill in quill and beadwork had been handed down from generation to generation within the

Plate 32. Beaded saddle blanket

family, the older Sioux women teaching the girls. At the time of puberty, maidens were expected to give up the freedom of early childhood and work quietly for hours each day on one of the handicrafts which the tribe had made its own. Sioux women now had new occupations and access to new materials.

Beadwork however continues to be carried on here and there through a wide territory. New pieces are shown at the annual fairs, at the dances where native customs are followed, and on Memorial Day when choice beadwork is sent to those who have been bereaved during the year. The desire to possess a handsomely embroidered costume exists among most of the older Sioux Indians. In some localities organized effort is being made to have the girls and the younger women continue the work so that knowledge of their native designs and of the technique of an art peculiar to their race will not be entirely lost. It was introduced as an elective at the Oglala Community School at Pine Ridge a few years ago, taught by a skilled Sioux woman whose training came from her grandmother. The girls were interested, the work was continued and is now being encouraged among the students of many of the Sioux schools of South Dakota.

Modern beadworkers have an almost unlimited choice of beads. The pony bead type is no longer used but seed beads are or were imported by wholesalers from Venice, Czechoslovakia, France, England, and Japan. The sizes and method of packing still remain similar to that previously described. Beadworkers judge beads to be purchased not only by their color but by the evenness and uniformity of beads on a string. At present, they use the larger size of seed beads rather than the extremely small ones found in the old work. They also use many cut glass beads which are less expensive but whose shiny effect did not please the old workers. Workers who realize the variety of shapes and colors now at their disposal have an interesting opportunity to develop the traditional style in new directions and for new purposes.

Beadwork Technique

When Indian women first obtained beads for their embroidery, they sewed them to the buckskin in two ways. One of these prevailed among all the beadworkers of the American continent and, though it was never much used by the western Sioux, we shall describe it first since its wide use suggests that it may have been the earlier of the two.

Overlaid or Spot Stitch. The technique of this stitch is substantially the same as that of quill work, i.e. a thread of sinew strung with a few beads is attached to the buckskin by another sinew thread sewed across it, just as formerly a thread was sewed across a quill. Couching is the name given by

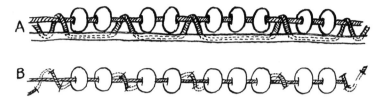

Figure 10. Detail of overlaid stitch: A. cross section; B, looking down. The dotted lines show where the sewing thread turns under the surface of the material.

white seamstresses to this method of attaching a narrow decoration without piercing it. Figure 10, above, shows the method in detail. Two threads are used, which we call the bead thread and the sewing thread. The end of the bead thread is attached to the buckskin, then the thread is strung with one, two, or possibly more beads and laid along the buckskin as the pattern demands. If the beads are all of the same color, there may be as many as six or eight. Then the sewing thread is stitched over it at right angles and into the buckskin where it is carried along, as shown by the dotted lines, until a few more beads have been strung on the bead thread and the sewing thread emerges and is stitched across it. The beads, closely pushed together, conceal both threads entirely. The number of beads strung on the bead thread before it is stitched down depends on the fineness of the work and whether it has sharp curves.

With fine work and curves, the sewing thread may cross after every two beads; with coarser work and straight lines, after three beads, four or even more. Elaborate flower patterns may be made in this way and also all-over work where a curving design is executed and then the background filled with closely laid lines of beads, straight or curving. It is an excellent stitch for floral patterns and was the one used by the Woodland Indians whose designs are of this sort. It is also used entirely by the Blackfoot, Sarsi, Plains, Cree, Flathead and in part by the Crow, Shoshoni, Assiniboin and Gros Ventre. Among the Sioux, there is a division. The eastern Sioux, who use floral patterns, naturally use the overlay stitch. The western Sioux use a stitch common on the Plains.

Lazy Stitch. The western Sioux, it has been mentioned, used geometric patterns for which the painstaking overlay stitch was unnecessary. They and the Plains Indians immediately around them, such as the Crow, Cheyenne and Arapaho, worked out another method suited to straight lines which has

Figure 11. Detail of lazy stitch: A, cross section; B, looking down—dotted lines indicate turn of thread under surface of the material; C, same as B, but with beads separated to show more clearly.

acquired the name of the lazy stitch.

Detail of the lazy stitch is shown in Figure 11. Here a given number of beads from six to twelve are strung upon a thread of sinew which has been fastened to the skin by inserting it in a perforation made by an awl. Another perforation is made to admit the sinew at the end of the row of beads. As in the overlay stitch, the perforation does not pass through to the underside of the skin but runs horizontally just below the surface so that no stitches show. The same number of beads is again strung on the sinew which is carried back to the starting point and passed through another perforation close to the first one. Thus the pattern is made up of beads sewed down only at the ends of each row. The strings of beads tend to arch a little between the stitches and a ridged effect results. In an all-over pattern these rows of parallel ridges make it easy to recognize any beadwork from the central Plains. They are somewhat wider than the bands which composed an all-over pattern in porcupine quillwork and yet they are very reminiscent of that former style. Though the sewing method is different from that of quillwork, it may be that Sioux women had come to like the banded effect.

Their stitch may have acquired its nickname of lazy because it is less firm than the overlaid stitch, and beadwork in which it is used is said to pull out sooner. However, it is an easy method of covering large spaces and, perhaps as a consequence, we find that the western Sioux often covered the whole of a moccasin or a dress yoke with solid color. Some Indians using the overlay stitch also made solid backgrounds, though with them the surface was smooth and showed no ridges. Both in texture and pattern, such work is entirely different from the products of the western Sioux with their clear cut geometrical figures and the even ridges which form a rhythm through the whole. Plate 33, p. 63 shows examples of both stitches.

Cloth and Thread

About 1850, traders began to bring cloth and velvet into Sioux country. Beadworkers welcomed the bright colors of the new fabrics and used them lavishly. But they and their near neighbors in the west central Plains were

Plate 33. Examples of overlaid stitch and lazy stitch

conservative in the use of materials. Commonly they continued to sew their beads to buckskin and then attached the buckskin to cloth. Many examples of the appliqué can be seen in blankets, leggings, bags, and pipe bags.

As long as beads were applied to buckskin, the thread used was generally sinew but when, in recent years, they were sewed directly on cloth, the thread was cotton or, more rarely, linen. Cloth, being of less firm texture than buckskin, brought about one change in technique. That is, the sewing perforations now passed all the way through the material so that the stitches showed on the wrong side. Many of the most elaborate and brilliantly colored examples of Sioux beadwork date from this later period when the beads were laid lavishly on backgrounds of red or blue cloth or black velvet.

While cotton thread does not wear well, a waxed linen thread is an excellent substitute for sinew.

Weaving

In early days, western Sioux women did not weave either quills or beads. Weaving was an eastern art, practiced by the Woodland Indians and, occasionally, by the eastern Sioux. The weaving frame used by these early weavers was a bow with a number of wrap strings strung on it in the position of the bow string and with perforated pieces of birchbark used as spreaders. In time, an oblong wooden frame took the place of the bow and this frame has finally found its way to the western Sioux. It was introduced, as far as is

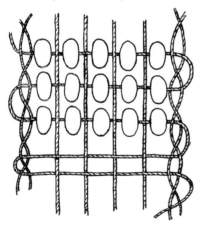

known, by white teachers in the Indian schools but has become popular lately for articles made for sale. Bead weaving by this method is an easier and quicker process than any method of sewing and it is also well adapted to the Sioux geometrical style.

Woven beadwork was used for headbands, armbands, scarfs, garters and belts. Strong cotton threads forming the warp are wrapped around the frame to the

Figure 12. Bead weaving—single weft

desired width. Beads are then strung with a fine needle on a thread that corresponds to the weft, and woven into the warp threads until the desired length is obtained. Then the warp threads are cut and trimmed into end fringes.

The weft may be single or double. In single weft (*Figure 12, p. 64*) a single thread, strung with beads, is passed in and out of the stretched warp, a bead being placed upon it between each two warp threads. In double weft, (*Figure 13, above*) the weft is strung with beads

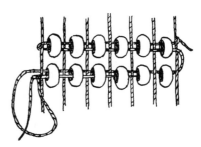

Figure 13. Bead weaving—double weft

and laid across the whole width of the warp, so that one bead appears between each two warp threads. Then the needle and thread are passed back through each bead on the other side of the warp.

DEVELOPMENT OF SIOUX DESIGNS

I N the early development of beadwork among the Plains and Woodland Indians, there were distinct geographic areas in which two types of decorative designs were used. Semi-conventionalized floral designs were used by the workers in the region about the Great Lakes, and geometric forms were developed by those in the area of the Great Plains.

The history of the Sioux quill and beadwork is one of constant movement. From the first sewing of quills, through the coarse "pony" beads and the fine seed beads, through backgrounds of buckskin or fabric, through sinew and thread, there has been frequent change of materials and, with each change, an adaptation of design. But designs have changed not only because materials changed. New ideas were constantly reaching the Sioux woman from the work, first of other Indians and then of whites. Her habit of using geometric figures did not change, whether from taste or from some ceremonial tradition we do not know. But the kind of figure she used changed several times, just as it is still changing. Those who picture an Indian art as fixed in a mold could hardly justify themselves by the close study of any one art, and especially not of bead and quillwork.

Until 1830, quillwork predominated over beadwork. We do not know when quillwork began, nor can we put a terminal date to the quillwork period for a few women work in quills to the present day. Beads, though they had come in about 1800, were still rare. Quill designs were on bands, single or laid side by side, patterned with stripes, bars, small squares, concentric oblongs, and triangles. (*Plate 25, p. 43.*)

Beads had been coming in since about 1800 and the earliest known examples of Plains beadwork date from about this time. The first embroidery with pony beads was in long, narrow bands, looking very much like quilled bands and with the same designs of bars, oblongs and rectangles. (*Figures 14 and 15, top row, pp. 68-69.*) This repetition of quill designs in a new medium was found not only among the western Sioux but all over the Plains. Women did not begin to work out new possibilities with beads until this and another preliminary period had passed.

Seed beads appeared about 1850 and in the first years after they had become common, there was not much change. Designs were often exactly like those of the pony beads but to them were sometimes added other geometrical figures like those which women had been painting on the skin envelope, or parfleche. These were still geometrical but, perhaps because of the shape of the parfleche, they had run to very tall, slender triangles, not usual in bead-work. There is also a K shaped figure (*Figures 14 and 15, middle row*) which is common among the Crow and the Shoshoni. They may have taken it from the Sioux or the Sioux from them. We can recognize this early small bead period by the fact that the work is still in long narrow bands decorated with solid triangles, two triangles point to point in the shape of an hour glass, these same figures terraced, or with circles, crosses and oblongs. There is almost nothing else. This banding was used to decorate men's leggings and robes and blankets (*Plate 24, below*), also pipe bags, cradles, and saddle bags. It never died out but it was pushed aside by a sudden new style.

Plate 34. Beaded blanket strip

New elements of design appear about 1870 in what is termed the second small bead period, often differing from the old in fineness and delicacy of line. Characteristic figures are the thin line, terrace, and fork spread out on a solid background. This style is not used by all Plains Indians, as was the former one, but is confined to western Sioux, Arapaho, Cheyenne, Gros Ventre, Assiniboin, Ute and, to some extent, Crow. Eastern Sioux, at this point, separate from their relatives and adopt the floral style of their eastern neighbors (*Figures 14 and 15, bottom row*).

The suddenness with which the new style appears among the western Sioux speaks of some outside influence. We have no proof, at present, as to what the influence was, though Mr. F. H. Douglas of the Denver Art Museum has suggested an interesting possibility. These new designs he finds to be surprisingly similar to those on a common household rug, made in the Caucasus and much used in America about that time. Settlers moving west with

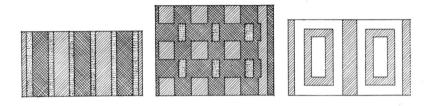

PONY BEAD PERIOD 1800 - 1840

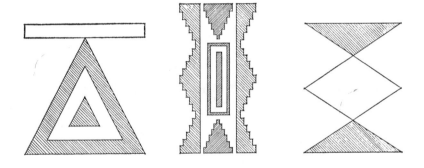

FIRST SEED BEAD PERIOD 1840 - 1870

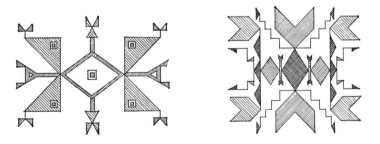

SECOND SEED BEAD PERIOD 1870 - PRESENT

Figure 14

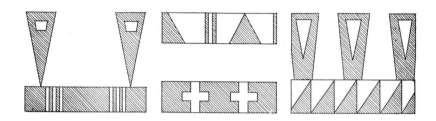

PONY BEAD PERIOD 1800-1840

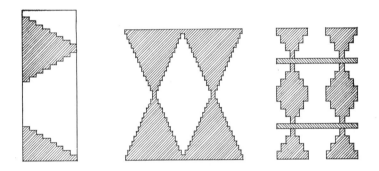

FIRST SEED BEAD PERIOD 1840-1870

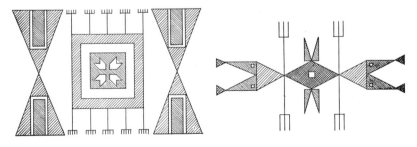

SECOND SEED BEAD PERIOD 1870-PRESENT

Figure 15

Designs in the "A" group are taken from Caucasus rugs, largely of the Daghestan type; those in the "B" group are taken from Central Plains beadwork. Both groups of designs are from the period since 1870.

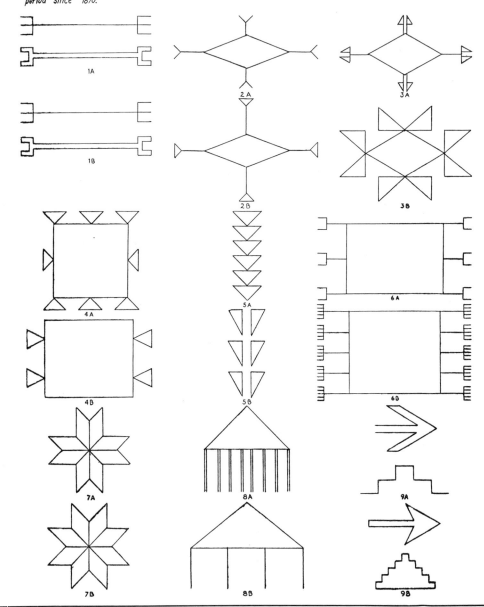

Figure 16

all their possessions, might well have brought such rugs. The Sioux or other Plains Indians might have seen them at houses or trading posts and, finding that the geometrical designs were not so different from their own, have adopted some of the new elements. Though we cannot feel sure that this took place, it is interesting to put a series of rug designs next to some Sioux beadwork designs from this period. This is done in Figure 16 opposite page, where designs 1-A and 1-B, 7-A and 7-B are identical, while the others show only slight differences. Since we know that eastern Indians, who used floral designs, often copied the flower patterns of the whites, it would not be out of character for the users of geometrical figures to copy new versions of these from the same source. History may reveal other sources as well but there remains the fact that the western Sioux, in the middle of the nineteenth century, began to use new figures in beadwork, which had not appeared in Indian work before.

The final style of Sioux beadwork, therefore, is a combination. It is distinguished, first of all, by an all-over, light-colored background on which appear three kinds of figures:

  a. Early, simple forms, like blocks and crosses, taken from quillwork or pony beads.

  b. Tall triangles and K shapes reminiscent of the parfleche.

  c. Delicate designs like those of Caucasus rugs with forks, lines and terraces.

The prevailing impression is one of lightness and openness. White is by far the most common background color, with medium or light blue next, and a scattering of other colors far behind. The figures are so spaced and colored as to give an effect of lightness, even when they are massive triangles and hourglass shapes. Their colors are usually red and blue, with green and yellow less common, and other colors scarcely appearing at all.

Since 1875, the trend in Sioux beadwork has been toward increasing elaboration. The strong, simple quality of the early work in small beads has given way to overcrowded patterns. About 1900, some workers gave up the old geometrical style and represented elks, men, horses, swastikas, which have no connection with their traditional designs.

Design Elements, Units, and Patterns

The Plains Indians have all used similar design elements and design units or motives in their beadwork. The straight line or narrow band, usually the width of several beads, has been used in simple arrangements since the days of the early porcupine quillwork. The lines are continuous, parallel, or crossed, occurring alone or as an attachment to other design elements. Joined at angles of different degrees, the straight lines are used to form the box, the rectangle, the dragon fly, the three-pronged fork, the full-of-points, and the horse track design units which form the basis of many of the Sioux design patterns. (*Figure 17, opposite page.*)

Equilateral, isosceles, and right-angled triangles are all popular design motives with the Sioux beadworkers. In the pony bead period the triangles were tall and slender. The triangles are used alone with apex pointing upward or in a few combinations that are often repeated. Two right-angled triangles standing on the same line, their acute angles facing each other, form a motive of common occurrence in the southern part of the Plains. In beadwork the triangles are necessarily serrated or stepped. (*Figure 18, p. 74.*)

With two isosceles triangles arranged base to base, a diamond or lozenge is formed. Sometimes the two triangles are given different coloring but more often are treated as a unit that becomes the center of an interesting design. A small rectangle, a pair of bars, or some other design is often enclosed within the diamond. Lines or triangles are almost always attached to two opposite corners of the diamond or to all four corners. Two right-angle triangles are quite generally used in this way. The trident form is used frequently in combination with two right-angled triangles and the diamond. Another much used motive in Sioux patterns is the "hour-glass" design where two equilateral triangles are joined at the apex.

Various design elements and units are combined in patterns for use on bags, costumes, moccasins, and other personal articles. Often the designs are symmetrically doubled and fill the entire space, as on the side of a bag. These elaborate patterns have come into use since 1875 after the use of the fine seed beads had been well established and after the introduction of Caucasus rugs.

In addition to the compact design pattern, elaborately built up by use of the design elements and units, the Sioux beadworkers used the design units separately. The box, the trident, and the dragon fly frequently occur on the field of blue beading on the yoke of a dress or on some other surface when enrichment of the background was desirable. The bag of an old chief might be decorated on one side with the feather design, denoting his rank, frequently repeated with no suggestion of pattern in its arrangement and on the other side with horse tracks, indicating successful raids, scattered over the beaded surface.

Sioux designs are made up of straight lines, continuous, crossing, or joining at angles of different degrees, chiefly right angles. The line designs are usually the width of several beads, determined by the size of the article.

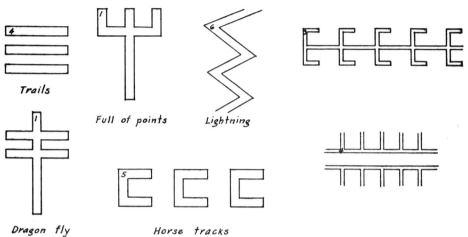

Trails

Full of points   Lightning

Dragon fly   Horse tracks

Squares and rectangles are much used in Sioux designs, frequently surrounded, entirely or in part, by a border of contrasting color

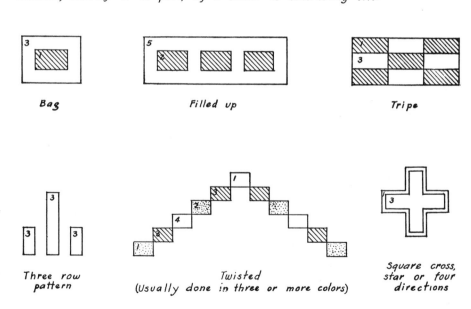

Bag   Filled up   Tripe

Three row   Twisted   Square cross,
pattern   (Usually done in three or more colors)   star or four
                                                          directions

Figure 17   73

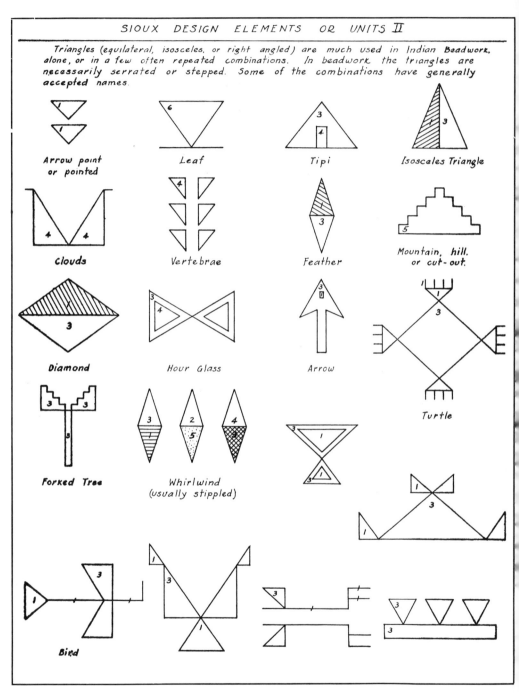

SIOUX DESIGN ELEMENTS OR UNITS II

Triangles (equilateral, isosceles, or right angled) are much used in Indian **Beadwork**, alone, or in a few often repeated combinations. In beadwork the triangles are necessarily serrated or stepped. Some of the combinations have generally accepted names.

Arrow point or pointed

Leaf

Tipi

Isosceles Triangle

Clouds

Vertebrae

Feather

Mountain, hill. or cut-out.

Diamond

Hour Glass

Arrow

Turtle

Forked Tree

Whirlwind (usually stippled)

Bird

Names of Designs

It has come to be common practice for beadworkers to call the most common designs by descriptive names such as star, tree, turtle, vertebrae, lightning, tripe, or rock. Some of these are old Indian names, though there is no evidence that they were standardized and used by all the beadworkers. Many names, though they refer to Indian surroundings, like the dragon fly, have been used only since the coming of the whites. Others, like the trident and hourglass, do not even refer to Indian surroundings. It seems most probable that the ancient bead and quillworkers, having worked out a design, noticed its resemblance to some natural object, like an arrow point, and then applied the name for convenience of reference. Often it must have been a white purchaser who gave the design a name. Since many such names have now come to be commonly used, it may be of interest to supply a short list of them (*Figures 17, 18, 19, pp. 73, 74, 77.*)

Design Elements Most Commonly Used by the Sioux

Bag, box or bundle — a small rectangle usually solidly beaded, often provided with a border beaded in contrasting color.

Cut-out — a graduated or stepped triangle or pyramid.

Dragon-fly — across with two bars.

Feathers — long, narrow isosceles triangles, joining others of equal size at the base.

Filled-in — parallel lines with small squares spaced between.

Forked or full-of points — three short lines or rectangles of equal length, joined by an arm to a longer stem.

Horse-tracks — two short, parallel lines or narrow rectangles of equal length connected at one end of each by a third line of the same length to form a U shaped figure.

Leaf — an inverted equilateral triangle whose apex touches the middle of a straight line.

Point — a small, inverted equilateral triangle.

Three-row pattern — Three narrow rectangles in a vertical position parallel to one another, the center one longer than the two end ones which are equal in length.

Trails	— short, parallel lines of equal length.
Tripe	— a rectangle divided into small rectangles of equal size.
Turtle	— a diamond with forked designs or two small right-angled triangles facing one another at the opposite ends, lengthwise of the diamond.
Twisted	— a row of stepped rectangles, the lower corner of the top one touching the upper corner of the one below, which at the diagonally opposite corner touches the upper corner of the next one in succession.
Vertebrae	— two parallel rows of right-angled triangles facing in opposite directions with the right angles at the top a short distance from one another.
Whirlwind	— two elongated triangles of different colors, joined at the base forming a long narrow diamond; one half of the diamond is usually stippled or barred.

Designs as Symbols

Just as the Sioux beadworker often named her design after some natural object after she had looked over the finished work and noted some resemblance, so she sometimes used it as a symbol of some mystic idea or tribal scene. Because individual women occasionally used designs in this way there has grown up an impression that this was regular practice and that there was almost a language of beadwork capable of telling a complicated story which any Sioux would understand. This impression is not confirmed by inquiry among individual beadworkers. It seems rather, that each woman named her design as she saw fit and that what might be arrow points for one woman could be tipis for another or, in fact, could be anything which had a triangular shape. The design might be indeed a symbol, but only for its maker. There was no general beadwork language.

Design as Related to the Object Decorated

Decoration on quill and beadwork often served the purpose of covering seams or some other portion of a garment, and the form of the design was determined thereby. For example, meander or border patterns of repeated units were developed on the bands that extended from the shoulders down the front and the arms of the shirt or down the sides of the legs. Round designs

76

PATTERNS USED IN SIOUX BEADWORK WITH DESCRIPTIVE NAMES			
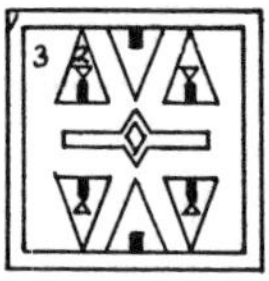	Complex tent design	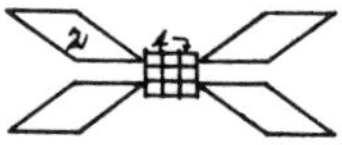	Rabbit's ear design
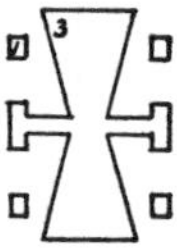	Cross built up of tent patterns	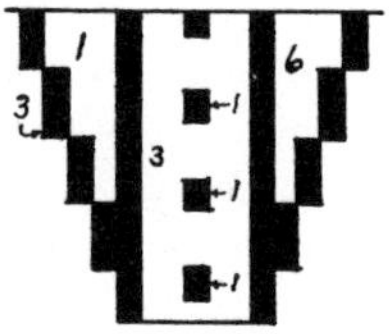	Reverse Hill
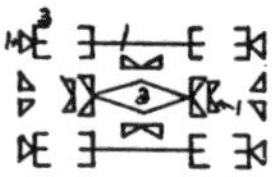	Dead mans body showing wounds and spears	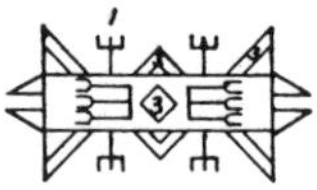	Shooting-of-arrows from between the hills
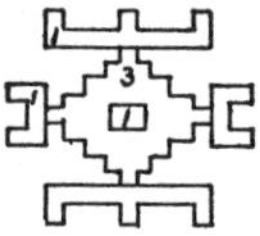	Full-of-points design	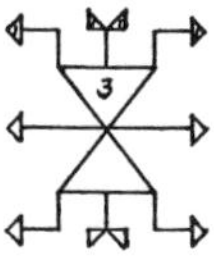	Spider design
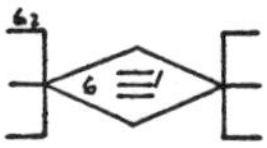	Horse-killed-in-battle	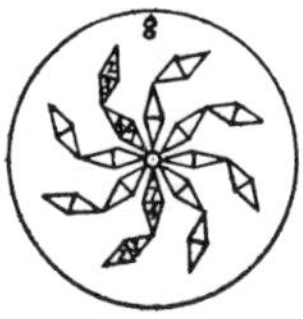	Whirlwind or Sunburst, enclosed in a circle to represent the world (Eastern Santee)
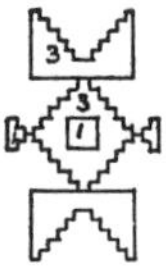	Leaf or Point design	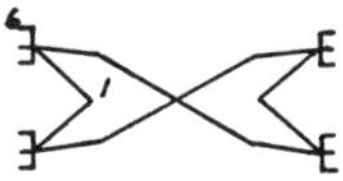	Hour glass with feather tips
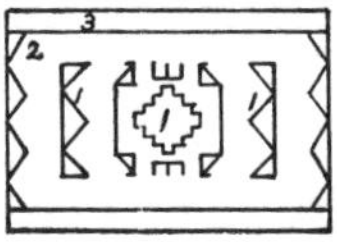	Looking glass or Reflected Pattern	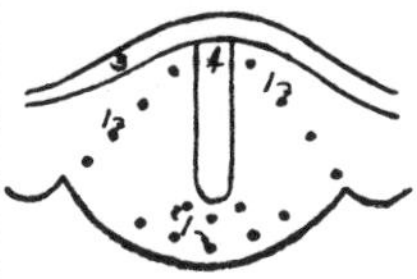	Breast of Turtle. The design used on yoke of a woman's dress.

Figure 19

were quite generally used on shields. Knife blade outlines were used on knife scabbards.

Some designs were used especially for objects used by men, other designs for objects used by women. Special designs were used on articles provided for special ceremonies and societies. The designs etched or painted on rawhide were distinct from those beaded on dressed skins.

To a considerable extent each article decorated had a characteristic design which bore some relation to the use of the article or the attributes of its owner. A design resembling a feather was embroidered on the bag made for the successful warrior to show his right to wear the sign of success in warfare.

The bilateral swallow design was used on saddle bags, one half of the design to show on each pocket. (*Plate 16, p. 28.*)

The horse track design based on the footprint of the horse might be used on tents or on the bag made for a brave man showing that horses had been captured from the enemy. It was usually made of straight lines, but sometimes the connected end is curved like the horse shoe.

The turtle design was used on the yoke of a woman's dress and leggings and at the head or side of the baby-carrier or cradle. The turtle was used as a talisman. The U-shaped design below the yoke of the woman's dress represented the breast of a turtle, the wing-like extensions corresponding to the sides of the shell. Used symbolically the turtle design had power over the diseases peculiar to women and also over birth and infancy. Turtle designs were worn only by women.

The spiderweb design when wrought on the robe of a child by a medicine woman was a symbol of power invoked for the future good of the wearer. Among some of the tribes the spider was mythologically regarded as the instructor of women in the art of embroidery.

Circular designs were used on shields, blanket bands, tents and on the large buffalo robes that served as ceremonial costumes in the old days. A large circular sun design made up of the feather element or motive and popularly known as the "black war bonnet," was painted in soft earth colors on many of the old robes worn by the men. The circular designs such as the medicine hoop or circle with a central dot were not used for decoration, but to invoke protection or for other symbolic purpose. Today circular shield designs are used as decorations on tents where the element of protection is symbolically invoked.

A special design might be adopted by any person as the result of a

Shield Design

An old porcupine quill design (arrow point) done in several shades, irregularly introduced.

Figure 20

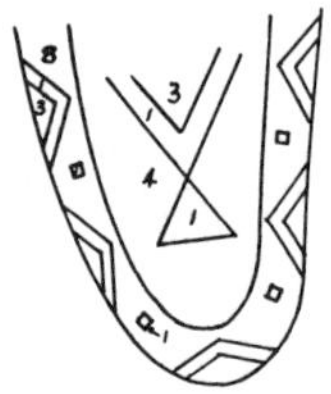

	Hour glass pattern. Tipi border
	Road, trail, or path pattern
	Cut out or step pattern. Filled up border
	Twisted pattern
	Middle row pattern with vertebra about border
	A space or part-between pattern Border – bundle, bag, box or rock pattern
	Feather pattern
	Feather pattern
	Tipi Border
	Hour glass pattern Border – forked design.

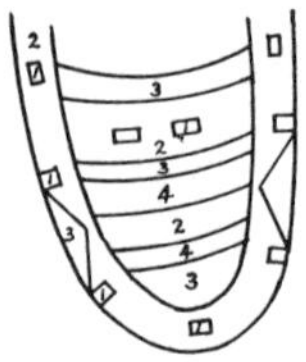

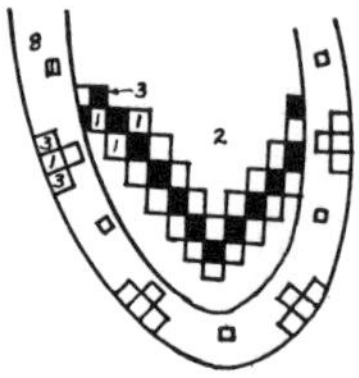

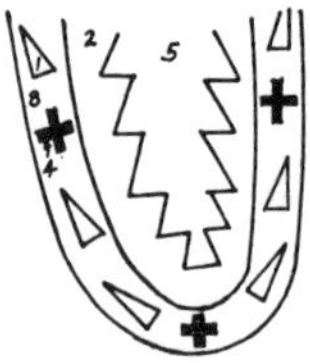

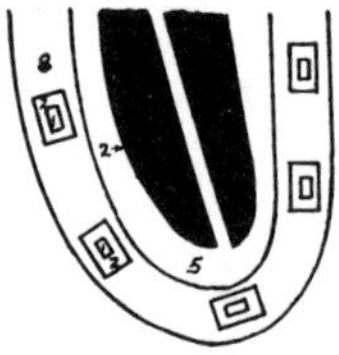

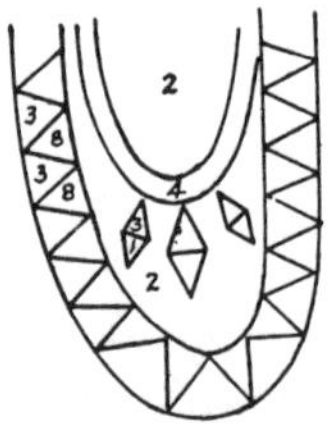

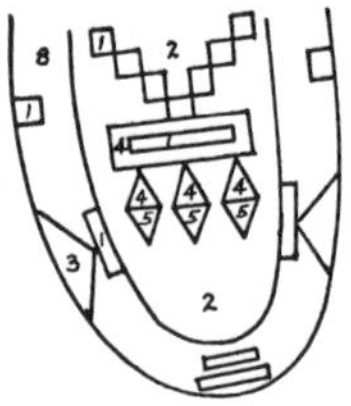

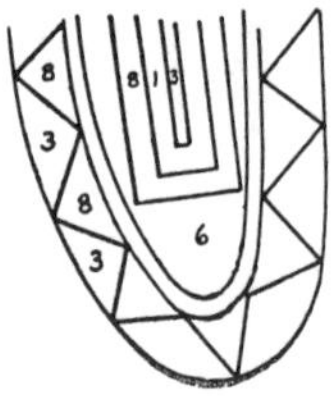

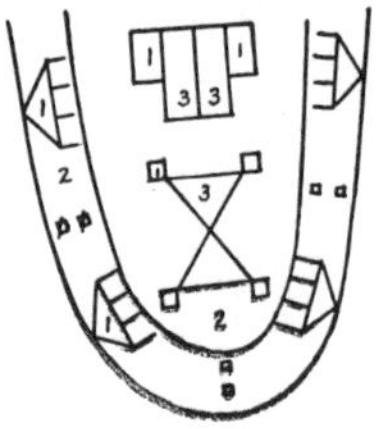

MOCCASIN DESIGNS USED BY THE SIOUX BEADWORKERS

Figure 21

vision or some important event or exploit. The eagle design might be chosen to indicate strong leadership. The tomahawk or the bow and arrow might be chosen to represent the fearless warrior.

Probably because of the limited surface available for decoration, specai designs have always been developed for moccasins. The Plains moccasin has generally been made up with a separate stiff sole. The soft top has offered a surface of peculiar shape which has usually been partially beaded, or not beaded at all if intended for daily use, or beaded fully if used on ceremonial occasions. The embroidery work on the upper, which is done before the sole is attached, has been characterized by the use of small geometric designs arranged symmetrically on a solidly beaded background of uniform color. An ornamental border about one-half inch or more in width in which conventional designs are worked out in colors is usually used all around the edge that is attached to the sole. A plain or beaded flap sometimes fell over the front or instep of the moccasin. The flap might end in two embroidered tabs as on the moccasins of the Kiowa.

Designs on moccasins were originally painted. A moccasin that was stained or painted green might indicate that the owner had gone on the war path in summer. If a man had been wounded, his left moccasin might be painted or beaded in black, the right one in red.

The designs most frequently used on Sioux moccasins are the tipi design, usually shown with a rectangular area, its narrow side resting on the base of the triangle; the blocklike pattern called the cut-out or step pattern which represents a hill; the rectangle enclosing a smaller rectangle called the bundle, bag, or box pattern; the double cross or dragon fly; the road, trail, or path pattern; the twisted pattern, which gives opportunity for variation in coloring; the filled-in pattern; the tripe design; the three-row pattern; the middle-row pattern with vertebrae about the border; and the pattern known as a space or part-between in which two duplicate patterns extend longitudinally to the toe of the moccasin. Smaller designs are usually seen on the women's moccasins which are built up higher than the men's moccasins so that they may be tied snugly about the ankle. A woman sometimes embroidered moccasins for a man on which the combined design elements represented a supernatural experience, his military accomplishments, or some other episode in the man's career. (*Figures 20, 21, 22, 23, pp. 79, 80, 83, 84.*)

An interesting development in the decoration of the moccasin is where the quillwork or the beading is carried entirely across a soft sole. The Sioux moccasins for service were made with stiff soles. The moccasins with the decorated sole were made to be used as part of the burial costume or to be worn by people of distinction on festive occasions.

Moccasin designs have always been made up with a wide range of coloring. A white or sky-blue beaded background is quite generally used. Yellow, orange, red, green, navy blue, and turquoise all appear in moccasin designs.

Use of Patterns in Making Designs

Though the early quill and beadworkers of the western Sioux used no patterns, carrying their designs in their memory and developing them as they worked, today some of the older women, as among the Sisseton, make designs by folding and tearing or cutting paper, thus assuring a balanced pattern. Folded and torn or bitten patterns may have been derived from similarly manufactured patterns of birch bark made by the Indians of the Great Lakes and eastern Canada. Patterns have proved necessary in recent years for the younger Indians to make marketable products.

With the wide latitude permissible in the use and arrangement of the Sioux design elements, the present day handicraft worker can develop attractive patterns, confining herself to the accepted geometric forms.

Colors Used

Beads made of seeds, shells, and other native materials were probably first used in their natural colors. Even with such a limited range, attractive color combinations were possible. Porcupine quills have been dyed by the Indians since very early times from soft colors obtained by extracting the dyes from plants. The soluble vegetable dyes penetrated the quills more evenly and produced more satisfactory results than did the mineral colors. As soon as commercial beads and dyes became available the quill and beadworkers of the various tribes showed a desire for more varied colors. The brighter red, yellow, purple, and green aniline dyes quickly replaced the softer native dyes in the quillwork, and bright colored glass beads rapidly became popular.

On festive occasions when the costumes were especially vivid, both men and women painted their faces with charcoal and vegetable or earth colors, often with a bright spot of vermillion on each cheek. Their striking light-colored beadwork with brilliant designs on a clear background formed a fitting contrast to the rich hue of their skins and their vivid paint. The native Indian paints and dyes included red, black, white, and various shades of yellow

BORDER DESIGNS OF THE SIOUX USED CHIEFLY ON MOCCASINS

BLUE OR RED ON WHITE BACKGROUND

Figure 22

84

Figure 23

and orange. Blue was much rarer and green was almost nonexistent, though it sometimes did occur. Until light blue came into use, white was almost universally used by the Sioux as the background color in their beadwork.

There is ample evidence that symbolism existed in the use of colors by the Indians, but the meanings varied in different sections of the country, in different groups, and on different objects and according to the ideas of different workers. It is therefore difficult to provide any generalized interpretation of either color or design. Some of the interpretations of color symbolism which have been recorded by scientists follow. They are not to be taken as regularly used meanings.

White, which during the last third of the nineteenth century became most commonly used for a background in Sioux beadwork, might signify snow or winter, the time of year when the men went on the war trail or achieved honors while the women carried on their handiwork at home. White and red might refer to personal qualities. White might also refer to objects in nature, especially objects which were consecrated—the buffalo, the deer, the rabbit, or the plumage of birds.

Blue is a favorite color of the Sioux though the pigment was probably not known to them until after the coming of the trader when it was at once adopted as a substitute for black. Blankets purchased from the trader provided one of the earliest sources of blue coloring. The women ravelled old blue blankets and boiled the yarn with their quills to make them blue.

Sky blue has been used to some extent by the Sioux beadworkers as a background color, particularly on the yokes of the women's buckskin or doeskin dresses where it may represent a lake or body of water in which the sky is reflected. This was called "blue breast beading." A sky blue background was also used in the beaded decoration on the baby's cradle. A characteristic of the beadwork of the Assiniboin, who separated from the Sioux about 300 years ago, was the use of the dark blue or purple background.

Navy blue or black may represent victory or enemies killed. In ceremonies, blue may represent the sky, clouds, wind, the west, lightning, thunder, the moon, water, and day. Black may represent the night.

Red has always been used by the Sioux on their faces as well as in their handicrafts. Red circles were painted on the face of the successful warrior. Red lines were sometimes painted on the face of the girl who had reached maturity.

Red on a weapon might indicate wounds inflicted; on a coat, wounds received. Only one who had been wounded in fight had the right to wear the red feather. One or more red lines were used across the center of the beaded feather design to indicate the number of battles in which the warrior had taken part.

In ceremonies, red might indicate sunset, thunder, lightning, or forms of plant or animal life. A red border was sometimes painted around the lower part of the tipi to indicate that those who visited there would be fed or that the tipi was one of a group in which a feast was to be held.

The red line, much used in both quill and beadwork, was known as the life span or "the trail on which woman travels," and was regarded as symbolic of that portion of a woman's life during which children may be born. Red lines or stripes on articles used by women were often associated with women's functions and virtues and symbolized the good life. They were used on the woman's parfleche bags, saddle cloth and saddle bags, on the girl's puberty robe and moccasins, and on cradle decorations for both boys and girls.

SUMMARY

SIOUX beadwork, as it exists today, is the product of two influences: Indian and white. The old quillwork from which it evolved was an Indian invention, unique in North America and practiced nowhere else world. But the materials and designs of quillwork were gradually abandoned as a new art evolved which was Indian in spirit but white in materials and, in some respects, in design.

We have seen how Sioux women acquired pony beads from the incoming traders and began to make the old quill designs in this new medium with new colors, blue and white. We have seen how they next acquired an improved and smaller bead which allowed them to cover larger areas with a wider color range. They were ready now for more elaborate patterns than the simple ones suited to the stiff, vegetable dyed quills. White trade goods suggested many of these patterns which appeared perhaps on rugs, perhaps on other textiles. But it was the art sense of the Sioux woman which selected and combined them in geometrical designs growing out of the ancient tradition. Finally, even the buckskin which had formed the basis of the early decoration began to be replaced by baize cloth and velvet while sewing thread replaced sinew. The background of the decoration, and sometimes the decoration itself, was directly imported from the white or stimulated by white influence. But that did not make beadwork a white man's art. No white, given beads and flannel, would be likely to work out the art style which came naturally to the Sioux woman who passed white man's materials through an Indian imagination. The result is an art deriving from both cultures and forming an interesting example of the interplay which has been going on between them through the centuries.

MUSEUMS

In which choice collections of Indian arts and crafts can be found.
(Many other State and municipal museums could be added to this list.)

American Museum of Natural History, New York City.

Brooklyn Museum, Brooklyn, New York.

Bureau of American Ethnology (Library), Washington, D. C.

Cleveland Museum of Natural History, Cleveland, Ohio.

Denver Art Museum, Denver, Colorado.

Field Museum of Natural History, Chicago, Illinois.

Sioux Museum, Indian Arts and Crafts Board, Rapid City, South Dakota.

Milwaukee Public Museum, Milwaukee, Wisconsin.

Minneapolis Museum of Arts, Minneapolis, Minnesota.

Museum of American Indian, Heye Foundation, New York City.

Museum of Anthropology, University of California, Berkeley, California.

Museum of Northern Arizona, Flagstaff, Arizona.

Museum of the State Historical Society of Minnesota, State House, St. Paul, Minnesota.

Museum of the State Historical Society of Nebraska, State Capitol, Lincoln, Nebraska.

Museum of the State Historical Society of North Dakota, Bismarck, North Dakota.

Museum of the University of Kansas, Lawrence, Kansas.

Museum of the University of Pennsylvania, Philadelphia, Pennsylvania.

National Museum of Canada, Ottawa, Canada.

Neville Museum, Green Bay, Wisconsin.

New York State Museum, Albany, New York.

Oklahoma Historical Museum, Oklahoma City, Oklahoma.

Oshkosh Public Museum, Oshkosh, Wisconsin.

Peabody Museum of Harvard University, Cambridge, Massachusetts.

Pettigrew Museum, Sioux Falls, South Dakota.

Rochester Museum of Arts and Sciences, Rochester, New York.

Southwest Museum, Los Angeles, California.

State Historical Museum, University of Wisconsin, Madison, Wisconsin.

United States National Museum, Washington, D. C.

BIBLIOGRAPHY

Alexander, Hartley Burr
  Sioux Indian Painting with Brief Introduction and Notes.
  Two portfolios each 25 plates in color 19½ x 15¼. Published by C.
  Szwedzicki, 22 Rue Louis de Coppet, 22, Nice, France. 1937, 1938.
  Part 1—Reproductions of paintings by Sioux Indian artists.   Part 11—The art of
  Amos Bad Heart Buffalo.

Boas, Franz
  Primitive Art.
  Harvard University Press, Cambridge, Mass. 1928.
  "An attempt to give an analytical description of the fundamental traits of Indian Art
  —and to determine the dynamic conditions under which art styles grow up." A page of
  Sioux decorative designs is shown (page 179).

  The Decorative Art of the North American Indians.
  Popular Science Monthly, October 1903, Vol. LXIII, pp. 481-498.
  A discussion of the relation of decorative to realistic representation of objects in the
  handicrafts of the Indian.

Canadian Institute.
  Porcupine Quill Work.   Invitation Quills.
  Fourth Annual Report of the Canadian Institute.   Appendix to the Re-
  port of the Minister of Education, 1891, pp. 23, 24.

Cleveland Museum of Natural History, Cleveland, Ohio.   Pamphlet
  Indian Homes.
  Shows the tipi.

Denver Art Museum, Denver, Colorado. Department of Indian Art
  Leaflet No. 2—Hide Dressing and Bead Sewing Techniques.
  Leaflet No. 7—The Buffalo and the Indian.
  Leaflet No. 19—The Plains Indian Tipi.
  Leaflet No. 24—Plains Indian Clothing.
  Leaflet No. 41—The Sioux or Dakota Nation.
  Leaflet No. 56—Colors in Indian Arts, Their Sources and Use.
  Leaflet No. 61—Symbolism in Indian Art.
  Leaflet No. 62—Design Areas in Indian Art.
  Leaflet No. 63—Indian Vegetable Dyes.
  Leaflet No. 73-74—Plains Beads and Beadwork Designs.
  Leaflet No. 77-78—Parfleches and Other Rawhide Articles.
  Leaflet No. 82—Tribal Names: Part 1.
  Ten cents a single leaflet. In addition to valuable information on the title subject,
  each leaflet gives one page of illustrations and a good working bibliography.

  Material Culture Notes.
  Reports from the Ethnographic Laboratory.
    No. 2—A Crow Beaded Horse Collar.
    No. 6—An Incised Bison Rawhide Parfleche.

Ewers, John Canfield
  Plains Indian Painting.
  Stanford University Press, Stanford University, California, 1939.

Farabee, William Curtis
Dress Among Plains Indian Women.
The Museum Journal, University of Pennsylvania, Philadelphia, Pa.
December 1921. Vol. XII, No. 4, pp. 239-251.

Gilmore, Melvin R.
Glass Bead Making by the Arikara.
Museum of the American Indian, Heye Foundation, New York City.
January 1924. Indian Notes, Vol. 1, No. 1, pp. 20-21.

Goldenweiser, Alexander
Anthropology.
F.S. Crofts and Co., New York City, N.Y. 1937. Chap. XII, Indian Art,
pp. 171-179. 8 plates.

Hall, H. U.
A Buffalo Robe Biography.
The Museum Journal, University of Pennsylvania, Philadelphia, Pa.
1926. Vol. XVII, No. 1, p. 5.

Hodge, Frederick W.
Handbook of the American Indian.
Bulletin No. 30, Vol. I (1907) and Vol. II (1910). Bureau of American
Ethnology, Smithsonian Institution, Washington, D.C.
Arts and Industries. O.T. Mason, Vol. I. pp. 97-99.
Beadwork. Kroeber and Mason. Vol. I, pp. 137-139.
Costume. Walter Hough. Vol. I, pp. 310-313.
Moccasin. Chamberlain and Hough. Vol. I, pp. 916-917.
Parfleche. James Mooney. Vol. II, p. 203.
Quillwork. Alice M. Fletcher. Vol. II, pp. 341-342.
Rawhide. Walter Hough. Vol. II, pp. 356-357.
Skins and Skin Dressing. James Mooney. Vol. II, pp. 591-594.

Holmes, William H.
Art in Shell of the Ancient American.
Beads. pp. 219-297, Second Annual Report, Bureau of American Eth-
nology, Smithsonian Institution, Washington, D.C. 1880-1881.

Hough, Walter
**Racial Groups and Figures in the Natural History Building of the
United States National Museum.**
Smithsonian Report 1920. Washington, D.C. Miscellaneous Collection,
Publication 2647, pp. 624-627. Plates 21-27 and 30.

Illustrates Indian costumes and manner of living and shows application of designs to
various articles. Out of print.

Krieger, Herbert W.
**Aspects of Aboriginal Decorative Art in America Based on Specimens
in the United States National Museum.**
Smithsonian Institution Report 1930. Washington, D.C., pp. 519-556
(with 37 plates).

Kroeber, A. L.
The Arapaho Indians.
Bulletin, American Museum of Natural History, New York City. 1902. Vol. XVIII, Part I. Decorative Art and Symbolism, pp. 36-150. Out of print.

Of value in comparative study.

Decorative Symbolism of the Arapaho.
American Anthropologist, new series, Vol. III, No. 2, pp. 308-336. 1901.

Of value in comparative study.

Ethnology of the Gros Ventre.
Anthropological Papers of the American Museum of Natural History, New York City. 1908, Vol. I, Part IV, pp. 151-179. Decorative Art of the Plains Indians.

A comparison of designs and handicraft articles of various tribes with extensive notes on parfleche painting and a page giving the design elements for bead and quill embroidery and other illustrations.

Lowie, Robert H.
Crow Indian Art.
Anthropological Papers of the American Museum of Natural History, New York City. 1922. Vol. XXI, Part 4.

Extensive notes showing connection and contrast between Sioux and Crow beadwork and parfleche painting. pp. 273-322.

Merwin, B. W.
The Art of Quillwork.
Museum Journal, University of Pennsylvania, Philadelphia, Pa. 1918, Vol. IX, No. 1, p. 50.

Six plates, one colored.

Mooney, James
The Ghost-Dance Religion and the Sioux Outbreak of 1890.
Bureau of American Ethnology, Washington, D.C. 14th Annual Report. Part II, pp. 653-1110.

A limited number of colored plates showing painted shirts and native paintings of the Ghost dance.

Orchard, William C.
Beads and Beadwork of the American Indians.
A study based on specimens in the Museum of the American Indian, Heye Foundation, New York City. 1929. Contributions, Vol. II. $2.50.

Deals only with bead types and techniques.

The Technique of Porcupine Quill Decoration Among the North American Indians.
Museum of the American Indian, Heye Foundation, New York City, 1916. Vol. IV, No. 1. Out of print.

Salomon, Julian Harris
The Book of Indian Crafts and Indian Lore.
Harper and Brothers, New York City. 1928, $3.50.

A well-illustrated book including simple directions for making the articles described so that the boy or girl can learn something of Indian handicrafts.

Sloan, John and LaForge, Oliver

Introduction to American Indian Art.

Illustrated. Published by the Exposition of Indian Tribal Arts, Inc. 1931. Purchased through Mrs. John Sloan, 222 West 23rd Street, New York City.

Part 1. Beadwork. pp. 22, 23. Part 11. Includes articles on Indian Porcupine Quill and Beadwork. (Orchard).

Speck, Frank G.

Notes on the Functional Basis of Decoration and the Feather Technique of the Oglala Sioux.

Indian Notes. Vol. 8, No. 1, January 1928. Museum of the American Indian. Heye Foundation, New York City.

Spier, Leslie

An Analysis of Plains Indian Parfleche Decoration.

University of Washington Press, Seattle, Washington. Publications in Anthropology, Vol. I. pp. 89 et seq. 1925.

A comparison of the designs used in parfleche decoration by the various tribes with emphasis on the points of resemblance in the designs. No illustrations.

Plains Indian Parfleche Designs.

University of Washington Press, Seattle, Washington. Publications in Anthropology, Vol. IV, No. 3. pp. 293-322. December 1931.

Sixteen pages are devoted to illustration of parfleche bags. Seven Sioux parfleche designs are shown.

Wissler, Clark

The American Indian.

Oxford University Press, New York City. Third Edition, 1938. Chapter V. pp. 76-101.

Decorative designs.

Costumes of the Plains Indians.

Anthropological Papers, American Museum of Natural History, New York City. 1915. Vol. XVII. Part II.

Decorations of Plains Skin Dresses.

Photograph of dress. Journal, American Museum of Natural History, New York City, 1912. Vol. 12, No. 2, p. 66.

Decorative Art of the Sioux Indians.

Bulletin, American Museum of Natural History, New York City. Vol. XVIII, Part III, pp. 231-278. 1905. Out of print.

A valuable and well-illustrated article showing the design elements of the Sioux and describing typical decorative designs and their uses.

Distribution of Moccasin Decoration Among the Plains Tribes.

Anthropological Papers of the American Museum of Natural History, New York City. 1927. Vol. XXIX, Part I.

A study of "the way in which that trait has spread and with the correlation of both geographical and analytic methods of approach."

Indian Beadwork.

The American Museum of Natural History, New York City. 1919. Guide Leaflet No. 50. pp. 1-31.

A pamphlet of 31 pages with description and 25 illustrations of the technique employed in bead and quillwork and types of bead weaving of the Indians around the Great Lakes and on the Western Plains. The illustrations include a series of design motives from typical Plains Indians' beadwork, a page of which is devoted to the design elements used by the Sioux.

Indian Costumes in the United States.

American Museum of Natural History, New York City. 1931. Guide Leaflet No. 63.

Takes up geographical variations in American Indian costume-materials, patterns and decoration.

Indian Tailoring and Adaptation of Material to Use.

Journal, American Museum of Natural History, New York City, N. Y. 1916. Vol. 16, No. 7, p. 465.

Material Culture of the Blackfoot Indians.

Anthropological Papers. American Museum of Natural History, New York City, N.Y. 1910. Vol. V, No. 1, pp. 1-176.

North American Indians of the Plains.

The American Museum of Natural History, New York City. 1934. Handbook Series No. 1. (2nd Edition) Chapter 4, pp. 127-133. Decorative and Religious Art.

A brief, popular presentation of the subject with limited bibliography.

Riding Gear of the North American Indians.

Anthropological Papers. American Museum of Natural History, New York City. 1915. Vol. XVII. Part I.

Some Protective Designs of the Dakotas.

Anthropological Papers. American Museum of Natural History, New York City. 1907. Vol. I. Part II, pp. 19-54.

A discussion of the symbolism of the protective designs used by the Sioux in shield designs, Ghost-dance designs (Ghost-dance garments), the Hoop, the Whirlwind, the Thunder, the Spider, and the Spider Web.

Structural Basis to the Decorative Costumes Among the Plains Indians.

Anthropological Papers, American Museum of Natural History, New York City. 1915. Vol. XVII, Part III.

Plate 35. Sioux Woman in Costume

FOLIO OF
SIOUX DESIGNS

COLOR KEY

Most Sioux designs make use of eight major colors, adding at times a turquoise blue and a darker red. These were usually worked against a background of white or light blue. The colors in which the following designs were worked are indicated with small numerals which correspond to the key below. These are placed in the spaces, or on the lines separating the spaces when these lines are themselves colored. When no color symbol is given, the line or space duplicates another which is keyed.

1. Light red.   5. Tan.
2. Light blue.   6. Green.
3. Dark blue.   7. Black.
4. Yellow.   8. White.

94

Figure 24

Figure 25

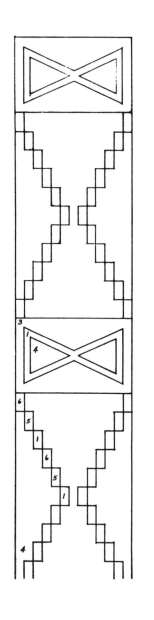

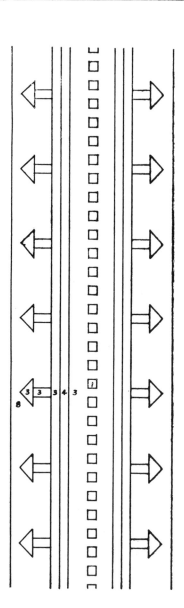

96

Figure 26

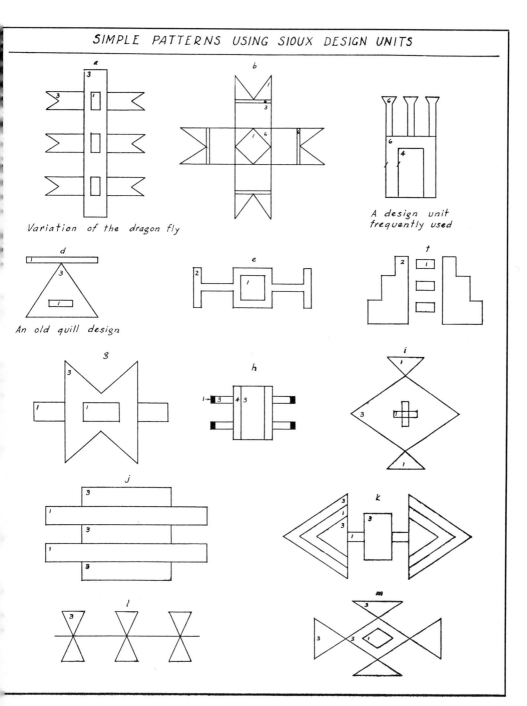

Variation of the dragon fly

A design unit
frequently used

An old quill design

Figure 27

97

Figure 28

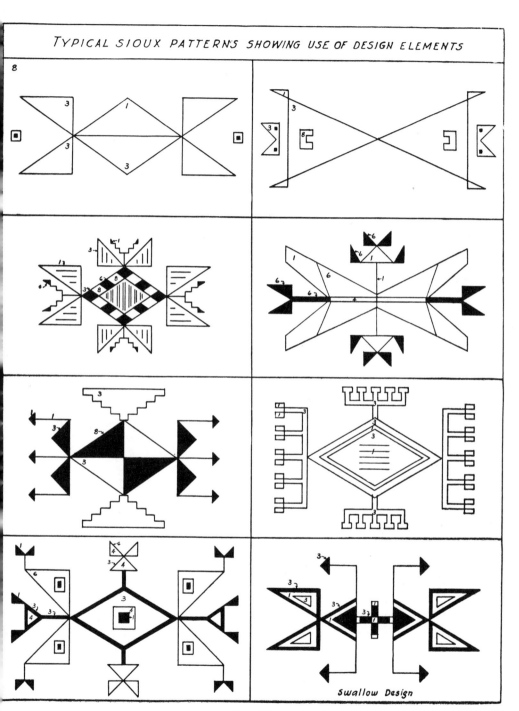

Swallow Design

Figure 29

99

Figure 30

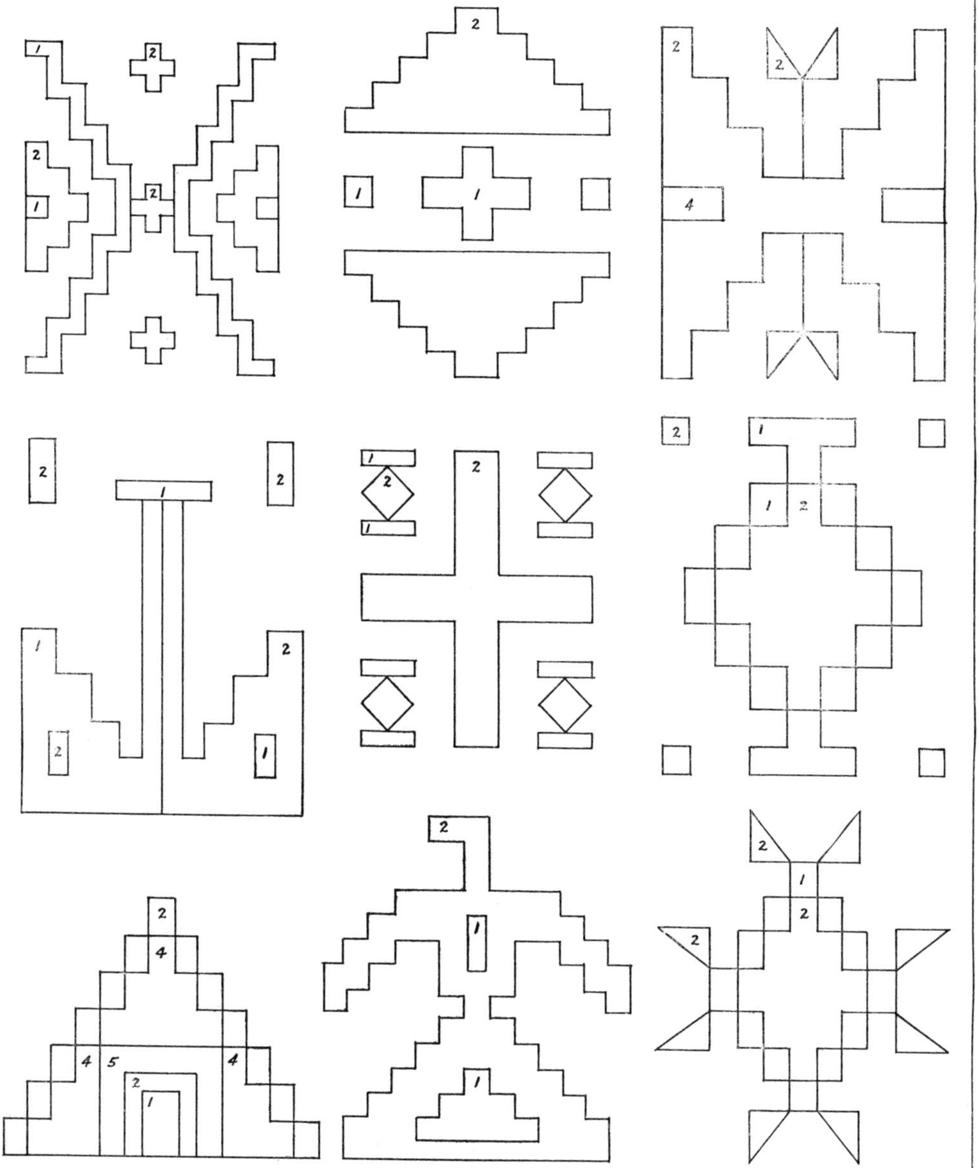

Figure 31

101

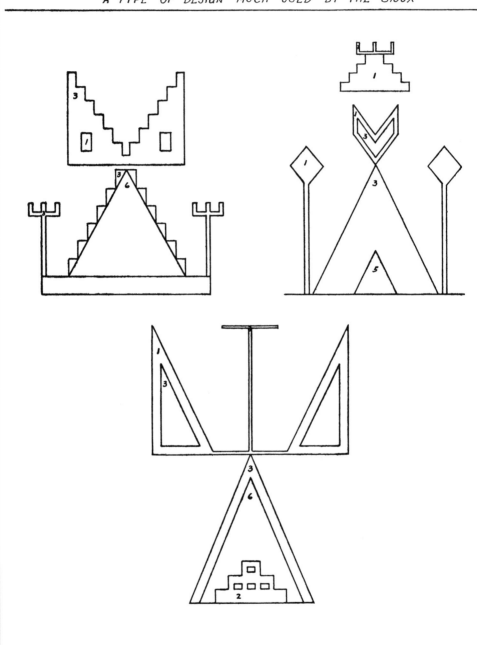

Figure 32

Figure 33

103

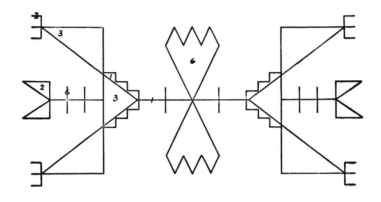

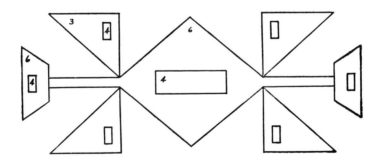

Figure 34

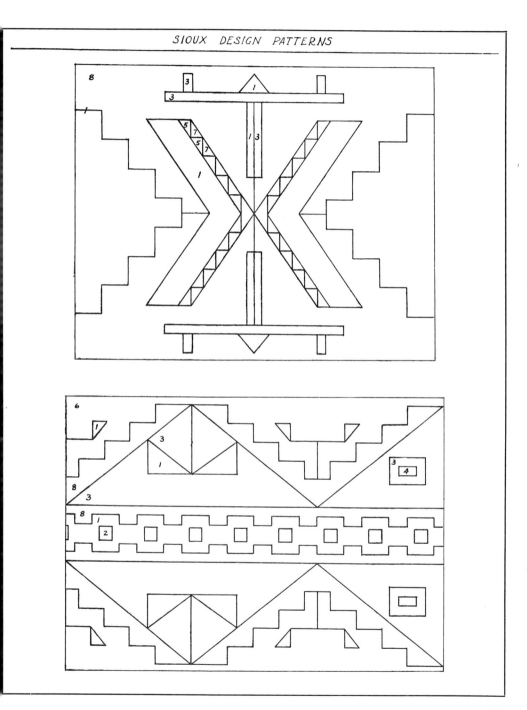

Figure 35

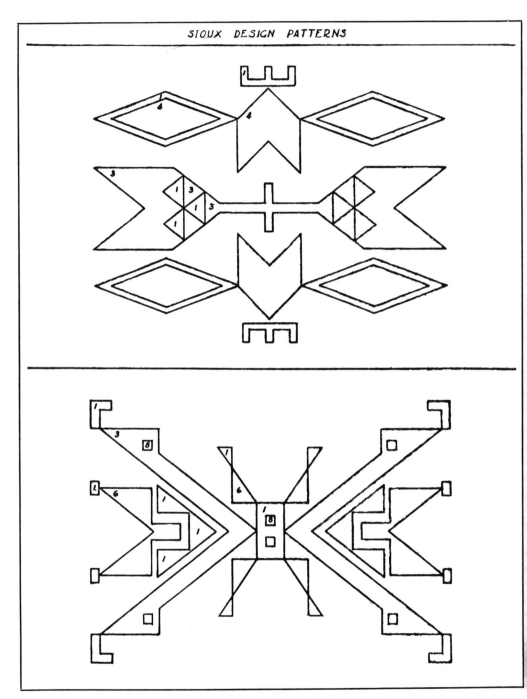

Figure 36

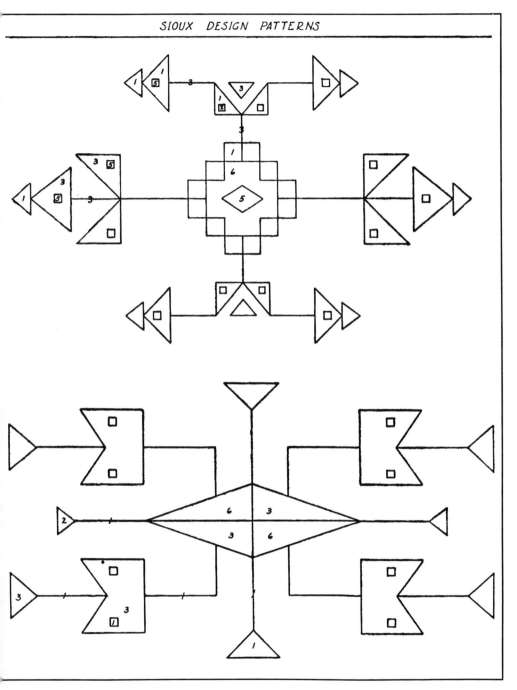

Figure 37

107

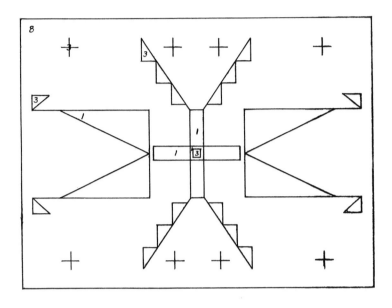

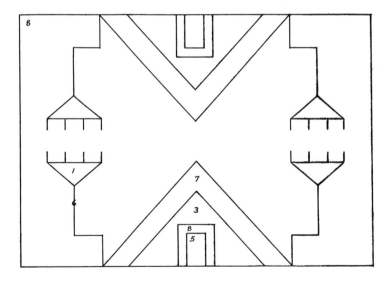

Figure 38

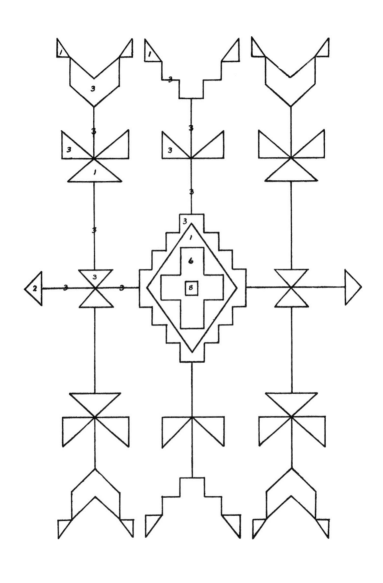

Figure 39

109

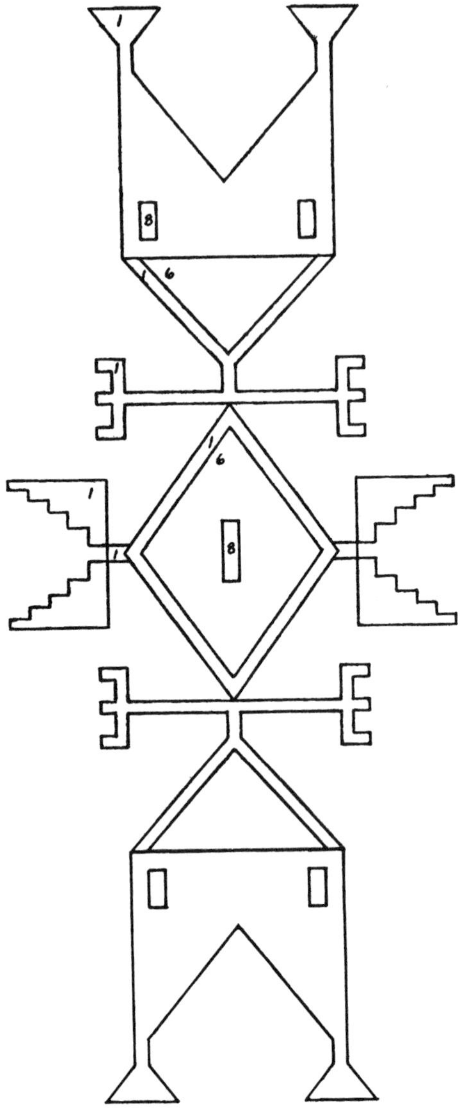

Figure 40

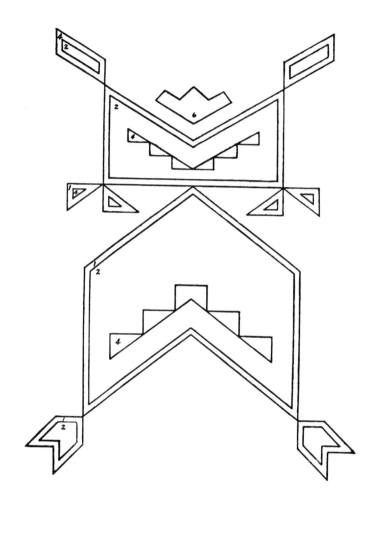

Figure 41

Figure 42

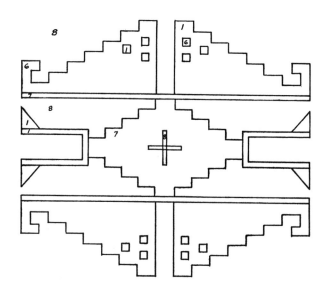

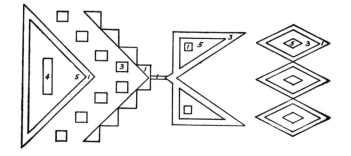

Figure 43

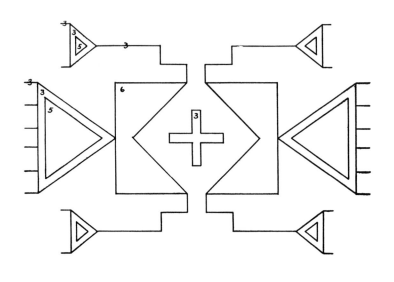

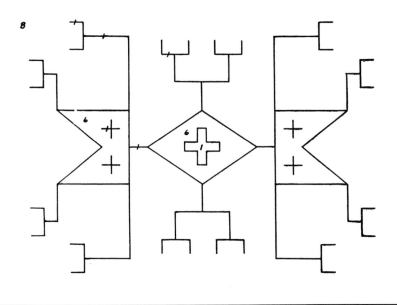

Figure 44

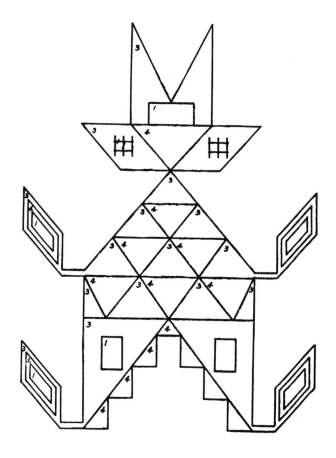

Figure 45

Figure 46